The 90 Minute Job Search Guide for Lawyers

A Book You Can Read in 90 Minutes

Erin C. Coleman, JD

The 90 Minute Job Search Guide for Lawyers
A Book You Can Read in 90 Minutes

Copyright © 2009 by Erin C. Coleman

ISBN 978-1-60910-011-7

Printed in the United States of America

Booklocker.com, Inc.
2009

To Gene, because you believe....

Acknowledgements

Thank you to all of those friends, family, and colleagues who have supported me, given me advice, and otherwise encouraged me in the writing of this book. Special thanks to my sister, Heather Coleman-Otuyelu and my boyfriend, Eugene Holmes.

Disclaimer

Contents

Why Listen to Me?

You might be asking yourself, "Why should I listen to her?," her being me, the author of this book. You still might not want to listen to me, but at least you will be able to make an informed decision after knowing my background. My legal experience, as well as my experience as an Assistant Director of Legal Career Services at a law school in Washington, DC, allow me to provide legal career advice based not only on research and past experience as a career advisor but also based on my personal experiences in the legal field over the past twelve years. In addition to being an Assistant Director of Legal Career Services, I practiced law in Tennessee as an associate at a law firm and in Georgia as an associate at a law firm. When I decided that I no longer wanted to be on the partnership track at a law firm, I looked for alternative ways to practice law or use my law degree. I was a Staff Attorney at another law firm, a Senior Assistant City Attorney for city government, a contract attorney, and a Staff Lawyer at a law firm in Washington, DC.

Not only have I researched alternative careers, I have had alternative legal careers. I was a knowledge management administrator in a law firm, and now I am an author. I have not been a law professor, but I did attend the Association of American Law Schools' annual conference where people are interviewed to be law professors. I also have interviewed for, and received an offer for, a visiting law professor position even though I did not take the position.

Since I have held many positions, I have gone through many job searches. I have even conducted long distance job searches. I conducted a long distance job search for a law firm associate position when I moved from Memphis, Tennessee to

Atlanta, Georgia. Before I moved to Washington, DC, I conducted a long distance job search from Atlanta, Georgia. And, since this job search wasn't successful, I know what it's like to move to a new city without a job. When I moved to Washington, DC, I did not have a job, but I did get a job once I lived there.

I have interviewed individuals for associate and summer associate positions at the law firms at which I worked and interviewed individuals for attorney positions at the city government for which I worked. While working at the law school in career services, I provided career advice to law students and alumni about job search strategies, resume and cover letter drafting, career resources, interviewing skills, and salary issues; conducted mock interviews; and conducted resume and cover letter review.

I am not just discussing topics in this book in the abstract. Many of the topics discussed are based not only on research but my experiences in these areas. For example, since I have been a contract attorney, the chapter entitled "It's Only Temporary: Contract Work" is based, in part, on my own experience. I have used some of the forms and techniques presented in this book to obtain positions in the legal field myself, so not only is this advice I would give to others, this is advice I would follow, and sometimes have followed, myself. I have had the sleepless nights, questions, confusion, joy, rejection, offers, increase in salary, decrease in salary, relief, and many of the other things that we all have when trying to decide what to be when we grow up and how to search for, and ultimately get, that "job of our dreams."

Why listen to me? Because, I've been there, and if I can make the job search process easier for you, all the better.

Use of Samples in This Book

You will find sample documents throughout this book such as a sample cover letter and resume. These sample documents may be used by you as a template to be marked up and modified for your job search. Please note that these sample documents are copyrighted.

INTRODUCTION

Have you decided that if you have to write one more memorandum comparing the statutes of limitations for filing a contracts claim in Delaware and New York, you are not sure you will make it to partnership? Does your position in the District Attorney's Office have no resemblance to *Law & Order*, and that's not a good thing? Do you want to save the whales, the trees, and the children, but being a lawyer for a nonprofit only makes you want to start another nonprofit called "Save the Bored Lawyers"? Put another way—Is it time for you to look for a new job? If the answer is "Yes," *The 90 Minute Job Search Guide for Lawyers* is the book for you.

No, you cannot in most instances complete your job search in 90 minutes, but you can read this book in that amount of time. As an attorney or any legal professional, you do not have a lot of time. There are many great resources out there about searching for and getting a job, but in the time that it takes to read these books, you could be searching for a new job. There are other resources that include self-assessment tools and a lot more information about finding happiness as well as finding a job; however, some of these resources are more than 300 pages long!! These books are often good resources and are in no way mutually exclusive with this book. In fact, there is a list (*Appendix H*) in this book that includes the titles of some of these books. However, if you have bills and student loans to pay, and you need a job yesterday, this is the book for you.

The 90 Minute Job Search Guide for Lawyers is for those who do not have the time or maybe just don't have the desire to read 300 or more pages. This is a bare-bones book with a few tips about searching for a job, accepting a job, and many of the steps in between. This book can be a starting point or it can be a refresher. For example, this is a book that you can pull out right before your interview for a few pointers before going into the interview without having to flip through hundreds of pages to find out whether you should ask about salary at the initial interview. This is more of a quick reference book, not an encyclopedia.

This book is written for the person who has never conducted a job search as well as those who have conducted several job searches. If you are the latter, do not be insulted by the suggestions in this book. To the more experienced job searcher, some of the suggestions might seem too simple to put down on paper. But, whether the suggestions in this book are simple or complex, my hope is that the suggestions are useful and helpful to you. For the first-time job searcher and the most experienced job searcher, this book is merely advice. You can follow it or not follow it—in the end—do what is most comfortable to you and what makes sense to you.

Simply stated, this is a book you can read in 90 minutes. This is *The 90 Minute Job Search Guide for Lawyers.*

Chapter One

What You Should Know Before Searching for a Job

You might not ever know what you want to be when you grow up, but have an idea of how you do and do not want to spend your day. Also, ask yourself and know the answers to these questions:

- Where are you willing to work geographically? Are you willing to move to a new city?

- How much money **must** you make?

- How much money do you **want** to make?

- Why are you looking for a new job?

- How long of a commute are you willing to have?

- What did you not enjoy doing day to day in your previous jobs?

- Do you want to work fewer hours?

- Are you looking for more interesting work and, if so, what does that mean?

- What is your "dream job"? Even if you do not get your "dream job" at this time, you can strive for it. You might get it or even come close. If nothing else, thinking about what makes up your "dream job" will help you to define what you are looking for in a job.

- What items are deal breakers? What will you not compromise on?

- What benefits do you want (e.g., health insurance, 401(k))?

- What kind of coworkers do you want?

- What type of office do you want to work in? Large, corporate office in the downtown of a city? Small office in the suburbs?

If you can't answer these questions, you might consider self-assessment books, or you might want to hire a coach. According to the International Coach Federation, coaching is "partnering with clients in a thought-provoking and creative process that inspires them to maximize their personal and professional potential."[1] I used a coach to help me to focus my career goals when I prepared to move from Atlanta to Washington, DC. It was very helpful to speak to someone who could be objective and offer me a fresh, unbiased perspective. Coaches can also help you to set goals and keep on track to accomplish those goals. Choose the career coach that is right for you. Additionally, it would also probably be helpful to choose a coach who understands lawyers and working in the legal field or a coach who specializes in helping lawyers. Although a career coach can be helpful, you might also consider other types of coaches such as life coaches. You do not have to limit yourself to career coaches. For example, if your desire to change jobs is just part of a larger desire to change everything in your life, a life coach might be a better choice than a career coach. For a good article on coaching and lawyers, see "Coach

---

[1] International Coach Federation, "WHAT IS COACHING," ICF—International Coach Federation, http://www.coachfederation.org/find%2Da%2Dcoach/what%2Dis%2Dcoaching/ (accessed May 15, 2009).

Me" by Jenny B. Davis in the June 2007 issue of the *ABA Journal.*[2]

---

[2] Jenny B. Davis, "Coach Me," *ABA Journal*, June 2007, 32.

Chapter Two

Where are the Jobs?
Searching for Job Openings

Job openings are listed everywhere. However, do not limit yourself to apply only to posted jobs. The following is a list of some of the places where you can find job openings whether posted or not. Some of the places are obvious such as the newspapers while others on the list are not so obvious, such as your mom:

- Internet: If you do not have access to the Internet, go to your local public library and use the computers there. *See Appendix A for a list of helpful Internet Web sites.*

- Newspaper (including legal newspapers): Again, if you do not receive the newspaper, go to your local library. *See Appendix B for a list of helpful newspapers.*

- Friends

- Family: If your mom is like my mom, she talks to everybody. She can be a good source for job leads. Not only your mom, but others in your family might have good job leads.

- Place of Worship

- Colleagues: These are the people who are in the legal industry. These are the individuals that you meet once a month in associations, such as your local bar association, or other groups. If you inquire about jobs from them, make sure they can keep your job search a secret, unless your job search is totally public. A totally public job search is one where the people at your workplace know of your job search, or if you do not have a job and there is no workplace to worry about. *See Appendix C for a list of associations and groups in the legal industry.* Many of these associations have job listings on their Web sites.

- Career Services (College or Law School): Check with the career services office of your college or law school and see if either has services for alumni. Some schools will provide free career advice, a job database, and other resources not only for current students, but also for its graduates.

- Legal Recruiters: A good legal recruiter, or "search consultant," or "headhunter" can be helpful in a job search given the correct circumstances. Make sure that you are not paying for the legal recruiter's services. You want to use legal recruiters that receive fees from the entity that hires them to search for a candidate. When deciding whether to use a legal recruiter, know that certain legal recruiters will only work with you if they believe that you are a possible match for the entity that hired the search firm. Also, consider whether you are more likely to get a job by applying yourself instead of using a legal recruiter. If Firm X can hire you without paying a fee (i.e., you apply directly), Firm X would prefer to hire you directly instead of paying a fee which can be several thousands of dollars (e.g., 25% of your salary the first year you are employed at Firm X)—especially in this economy. *See Appendix D for names of legal recruiters that may be helpful to your job search and titles of articles that discuss working with legal recruiters.*

- Cold Calls/Letters: This is the process of calling, or sending letters to, places to inquire whether there are any job openings. To do this, compile a list of places where you would like to work whether the places have specific job openings or not. If you send a letter, send a copy of your resume with the letter. You can compile a list of potential employers by searching legal directories such as Martindale-Hubbell, employers' Web sites, or any place where you can determine a contact person, the name of an entity, and what type of law is practiced at that entity. For example, if you are interested in practicing employee benefits law in Chicago, Illinois at law firms with fewer than 25 people, conduct a search on martindale.com by conducting an "Advanced Search." Choose "Law Firms" in the "Search For" section, and then you will have the ability to choose the city, the practice area, and firm size. This will give you a list of potential employers. Once you have selected who you would like to contact, call or send a letter and resume. For an example of such a cover letter, see the chapter entitled "Hello!: Your Cover Letter." The dialogue for the phone call can contain the same information as would be in a cover letter. Whether you call or send a letter, you can contact the person in charge of hiring. In a law firm, more than likely, that would be the hiring partner or the head of recruiting. Realize that you might be more successful using the cold call/letter method with certain employers more than others. For example, this is a sound method for contacting law firms; however, some government agencies that have a definite process might not respond to your letter, and if you call, you might be told to see the job advertisement and follow the process.

- Anyone who will listen!!: No, not really, but you would be surprised at some of the unlikely places that people learn about jobs. Your hairstylist might have just cut the hair of your future employer (who just happened to mention that she is looking for an attorney to hire). In this scenario, by letting your hairstylist know that you are searching for a job, she might be a source for a job!

In short, the job search is all about networking. The more people who know that you are looking for a job, the more information you can get about job openings. But, know your boundaries. Ask yourself: How many people do I want involved in my job search? If you are trying to keep your job search quiet, consider limiting the number of people you tell about your job search, and only tell people who can keep their mouths shut!

I have found jobs using several of these methods mentioned in this chapter: family, friends, legal recruiter, job posting on the Internet, and networking.

Chapter Three

Who Do You Know?
Networking

Getting Started

Make a list of every person that you know and let them know that you are looking for a job. Do not limit this list to people in your career field. Who do you know from work, your neighborhood, your gym, your place of worship, your grocery store, your family? If after you have exhausted your list of everyone you know, there are only three people on the list, do not lose heart. Contact your law school career services office. Ask the office if there is an alumni list that you may have. You might even be able to obtain a targeted list of individuals who practice in the city or area of interest for you. Ask the three people on your list who they know. They might know someone with whom you should speak.

After making the list, depending on how public your career search is, who must be crossed off of the list? For example, if you are not publicizing your search for a new job, you want to cross off of your list those individuals that cannot be discreet. However, you cannot be so secretive that your list consists of only two people. One of the benefits of networking is letting as many people as possible know that you are looking for a job. Do not assume that some of the people that you know might not be helpful. Your neighbor might not be a lawyer, but his best friend's son might know of opportunities in the legal field.

Although letting several people know that you are looking for a job can be helpful, you should make sure that there are individuals on your list in your area or job of interest. If you have some idea of what you want to do next, make sure that your list of contacts includes individuals in that field. For example, if you want to work in public interest law in Pennsylvania, you should include individuals on your list who work in public interest law in Pennsylvania. What are the organizations for which you would like to work in Pennsylvania? Would you like to work in Pittsburgh or Philadelphia or anywhere in Pennsylvania? Choose individuals with whom to network according to the answers to these questions.

Informational Interviewing

But, what if you do not know anyone who works in the field or the city that you are interested in working in? Now what? The informational interview is what. Although it is not easy to make cold calls, you can contact people that you do not know. Informational interviews work whether you know exactly what your next job should be, or whether you have no clue what is the next job, you just know you cannot stay where you are. They can work whether you know the interviewee or are meeting him or her for the first time. Distinguish networking through direct methods when you are letting people know you are searching for a job and asking them for help in that endeavor, and the informational interview where you are networking more indirectly for job leads. An informational interview is an information gathering interview, with the side benefit of networking, where the goal is not to obtain a job at the end but to learn more about the interviewee's job or career and related items about that job or career. If you do receive an opportunity to interview for a job, or if the interviewee offers to help you, that is great, but do not expect these items or ask for them. An informational interview can help the person who has known since law school that he wants to be a U.S. Attorney in Washington, DC or the individual who has decided that practicing law is not for him and is not sure what to do next.

After you have decided who to contact, prepare questions and an introduction to the individual. You can approach a contact via telephone, letter, or e-mail. Based on the relationship with the person and your comfort level, decide how to approach the person. You want to make the informational interview as easy as possible for your contact. Make clear that you only want a few minutes of his time at a convenient time for him in a forum that he wants. If the person does not want to give you an informational interview, scratch him off of your list and move on, but people often are happy to help you. Let the person know that you truly are conducting an informational interview even if there are no job openings at this time.

For example, Heather Parks is interested in securities law and wants to work in a small law firm or the local SEC office in Atlanta, Georgia. Heather knows Jennifer Jones who works at the SEC in DC and Jennifer knows an attorney, Jackson Sprat, who works in the SEC's Atlanta Regional Office. Heather calls Jackson (after speaking with Jennifer who suggested that she call Jackson and said that Heather could mention her name) and proceeds as follows:

Heather: "Hello, may I speak to Jackson Sprat."

Jackson: "This is he, how may I help you?"

Heather: "My name is Heather Parks. Jennifer Jones and I went to law school together at Georgetown University Law Center and she suggested that I contact you. I am presently working at Big Law Firm in the Corporate Department as an associate with a corporate and securities law practice. I am interested in working for the SEC in Atlanta, Georgia and was wondering if you would be willing to speak to me for about twenty minutes about the work that you do and any advice that you have for someone interested in working for the SEC. I would be happy to conduct this interview in a manner most convenient to you and your schedule."

Jackson: "I would be happy to speak with you. Why don't you call me tomorrow at 3:00 p.m."

Prepare questions for the interview. Ask questions that really interest you. You might not want to discuss salary at this time, especially if you can gather that information elsewhere. For example, listings for government jobs, like at the SEC, often include the pay grade or the salary range for certain positions. However, if salary amount is important to you at this point, ask the question. I wouldn't make it the first question though. *See Appendix E for sample questions you can ask in an informational interview*.

More About Networking

In addition to informational interviewing, there are other methods of networking such as joining local bar associations or committees in your area of interest. Attend seminars in your subject matter of interest. Do not carry resumes with you to these events unless the event is specifically a job networking event that requests that you bring a resume. You can always get someone's contact information and send your resume if so requested from the person. Whether networking through an informational interview or any other method, in most instances, do not offer to send your resume unless asked—otherwise, it is presumptuous. Remember, the individuals with whom you speak do not want to feel pressured into getting you a job. The person might not be a decision maker, there might not be job openings, or the person might not have the time. While the ultimate benefit of networking is to get a job, every networking contact will not result in a job directly from that contact, nor should it.

I know, I know—everyone hates networking. We lawyers are a proud people and we don't want to ask for anything, but to get a job—ask you must. Networking does not have to be an unpleasant experience. Be yourself and do not approach networking in a manner that is different from your personality (unless you are extremely shy, you might have to go out of your comfort zone). If you hate networking, go to Continuing Legal Education courses or association meetings that you enjoy. Go with the purpose of not only obtaining a job lead but learning something and meeting new people. It is possible that you will leave only with a new list of contacts. If the opportunity doesn't present itself at the meeting to talk about your job search, you can always follow up later. You must strike a balance between getting job search leads, being yourself, being somewhat comfortable, and not being pushy. Networking is an art that gets easier and better with practice. Remember, most people are happy and willing to help you.

In the end, you have to decide each situation separately. For example, if you need to get a job quickly, you might want to be more direct with your contacts by saying, "I am looking for an associate position, may I send you my resume?" In another situation, you might want to call a new contact for a combination of informational interviewing and direct networking: "I am interested in learning more about what you do and would also like to talk to you about any job openings that you might know about given that I am searching for a job in your area." By doing this, it takes the pressure off of the contact if there are no job leads but unlike the usual informational interview, it lets the contact know that you are looking for job leads. Also, if there are job openings, by talking to this person, if she likes what she hears, she might be able to help you in your search.

Networking works. I have gotten many of my jobs through some form of networking. Networking especially helps when you are new to a city. If you know anyone who knows someone in your new city who might be helpful to your job search, contact the person in the new city using the networking techniques described in this chapter. For example, when I moved to Washington, DC, I spoke to a contact of a friend. Let's call the contact "Ms. Nice." Ms. Nice contacted a contact of hers ("Ms. Helpful") to ask whether I could speak to her about my interest in the legal career services field. I spoke to Ms. Helpful about my interest in the legal career services field, and after Ms. Helpful suggested that I send my resume to her for a job opening, I sent it to her. She forwarded my resume and cover letter on, and I eventually got the job.

Chapter Four

Simon Says
Follow Instructions!

If applying to a job posting or ad, follow the instructions. Many of these postings or ads will state what application materials to include. For example, a job posting might provide: "Please send a copy of your resume with a cover letter by mail or by e-mail to hireme.com by March 2, 2009 for consideration. No phone calls please." If you are applying to this position, do not send a resume without a cover letter, do not fax your application, do not e-mail the application to any other e-mail address other than "hireme.com," and do not apply for the job on March 16, 2009.

Remember to follow instructions no matter how you learn about a job opening even if you don't learn about the opening from a job posting or ad. For example, if you learn about a job opening from a networking contact, ask if there is a job posting for you to follow instructions. If the job has not been posted, ask the person for instructions such as what materials are required and to whom to send the materials. Then, follow instructions.

There are exceptions to this rule of following instructions to the letter. For example, if you speak with someone at the employer's office with authority to affect the hiring decision for this job who gives you instructions that are different from the instructions in the job ad, follow what the person says. Let's say you call on March 16, 2009 and speak to the recruiting manager for ABC Law Firm and she tells you that the job is still open and that you can send your resume and cover letter to her—do so. You could also say in your correspondence: "As we discussed on the telephone today, please find attached my resume...."

Another exception to this rule is if someone you know through networking works at ABC Law Firm, for example, and has agreed to forward your resume for you. This can be very helpful if done correctly given that employers often receive hundreds of resumes, especially in this age of e-mails and fax machines. By having someone who works at the law firm forward your resume, this can separate your resume from the stack. Also, if this person is willing to recommend you for the job, that is even better. If you do this, find out from your contact if you need to also submit your resume by following the instructions in the job posting as well as have your contact forward the resume. For example, I applied for a job as requested in the posting, uploading my resume to the Web site, but also sent a copy of my resume with my cover letter to my contact to forward to the hiring decision maker after my contact suggested that I apply in this manner (apply as specified in the job posting and send resume and cover letter to contact for the contact to forward to the decision maker for me). Although I did not ultimately get a job offer, I did receive an interview.

Be careful in selecting who you ask to forward your resume. Make sure that person is doing well at the law firm and is not about to be fired himself. Make sure that the person to whom your contact is giving your resume is either the person making the hiring decision or will give it to the proper hiring person in the law firm. Although a law firm was used in this example, the advice in this chapter is true whether you are applying to a law firm, corporation, law school, or any employer. Just remember that the application process can be very different depending on who that employer is. A government application process can be different from applying at a law firm. Don't worry—as long as you follow instructions for the particular job you are applying for you will be fine.

If you are submitting applications to several places, you might want to keep a chart of the who, what, when, etcetera associated with your applications to keep it all straight. *For an example of a job search chart, see Appendix F.*

Chapter Five

Hello!
Your Cover Letter

The cover letter is your opportunity to introduce yourself and to explain not only why you want the job but why you are the best person for the job. It is an opportunity to pull from your resume those transferable skills that would be beneficial in the position sought. Although you want to express that you want the job and why you want the job, do not use the cover letter as the mechanism to express your job search wish list. Think about what you would want to know if you were the employer reading this cover letter and you were trying to hire a person for the position. Generally, not literally, tell the employer how you would make the employer's life easier if hired. Tell the employer why you are the person for the job. Do not merely state that you are the person for the job—support your statements with examples. Also, look at the job description. This can tell you what the employer is looking for as well as what credentials are needed for the position. Make sure that whatever you write in your cover letter, you ensure that you have used correct grammar, there are no typos, and the spelling is correct. Get a friend or family member to review the cover letter for you. Send the cover letter to your law school career services office if the office offers the service of reviewing cover letters and resumes. I promise, you can read the letter 100 times and not realize that you have stated that "I worked **their** for ten years" instead of "I worked **there** for ten years."

Make sure that your cover letter conveys what you want to convey but also is to the point and not too long. Your cover letter in most cases should not exceed two pages—one page is even better. Just as when you are meeting someone for the first time at a networking event you would not spend an hour introducing yourself, you do not need to have a five page cover letter. You want to grab the reader's attention and convey important information.

Include items in your cover letter that you could not put in your resume as long as the items are relevant to the job for which you are applying. For example, in certain industries, an "Objective" section is included in the resume. An "Objective" section might provide as follows:

> Objective: To obtain an associate position in a law firm in the Corporate Department.

For a legal resume, instead of including an "Objective" section, place that information in your cover letter.

If you are conducting a long distance job search, include information that indicates your ties, if any, to the targeted geographic area. For example, if you are living in Washington, DC and you are applying for a job in Atlanta, Georgia, if you were born in Atlanta, include a sentence such as the following: "As a native of Atlanta, Georgia, I am eager to move back home to practice law." You could also include in your cover letter times that you will be visiting the targeted city and a statement that you would like to meet: "I will be in Atlanta March 2, 2009 – March 9, 2009 and would welcome the opportunity to meet with you."

The following is a sample job advertisement and a sample cover letter in responding to this ad. Place the cover letter on high quality paper such as linen in a neutral color such as white or cream. This sample job advertisement will be the basis for other documents in this book, such as the resume and references.

Sample Job Ad

ABC Law Firm is searching for an associate with at least 2-4 years of experience working in a large law firm to work in its Corporate Department in the Atlanta, Georgia office. The candidate should have experience in general corporate law, securities, and mergers and acquisitions. Banking law experience is a plus.

Please send a copy of your resume with a cover letter and law school transcript by mail or by e-mail to Walter Coleman by March 2, 2009 for consideration. No phone calls please.

Walter Coleman
Hiring Partner
ABC Law Firm
1234 Symphony Way
Atlanta, GA 30309
wcoleman@ABCLawFirm.com

Erin C. Coleman, JD

Sample Cover Letter

HEATHER L. PARKS
1200 Music Street
Atlanta, Georgia 30303
(404) 111-1111
hp123@fakemailaddress.com

February 2, 2009

Mr. Walter Coleman
Hiring Partner
ABC Law Firm
1234 Symphony Way
Atlanta, GA 30309

Re: Application for Associate Position in Corporate Department at ABC Law Firm

Mr. Coleman:

I am writing to express my interest in the associate position in the Corporate Department at ABC Law Firm, in the Atlanta, Georgia office, listed on the ABC Law Firm Web site. My current position is at Big Law Firm as an associate in the Corporate Department in Atlanta, Georgia. Prior to that, I worked in the Washington, DC office of Big Law Firm in the Corporate Department. As an attorney who practiced law in the District of Columbia for two years, and in Atlanta, Georgia, I have gained experience that will allow me to make a substantial contribution to ABC Law Firm.

As you will find from my resume, my legal experience allows me to satisfy many of the requirements listed for the position of an associate at your law firm. At Big Law Firm, in addition to drafting and negotiating various merger agreements and associated documents, I recently closed the acquisition by my firm's client, a large national bank, of another bank. Additionally, I assisted in various aspects of the formation of state-chartered banks in Georgia. From the first day that I sat in my *Securities Regulation* course at Georgetown University Law Center to the Form 10-K I filed last week, I have enjoyed learning the intricacies of securities law and using that knowledge in my law practice. I would welcome the opportunity to join ABC Law Firm as an associate in the Corporate Department in Atlanta, Georgia where I can provide top-notch service to clients while working on sophisticated corporate matters only handled by a law firm such as your law firm.

Please find attached my resume and law school transcript. If you have any questions, comments, or would like further information from me, please contact me at (404) 111-1111 or at home via e-mail at hp123@fakemailaddress.com. I look forward to hearing from you. Thank you for your consideration of my application for the position of an associate at ABC Law Firm.

Sincerely,

Heather L. Parks

Attachments

As discussed in the chapter entitled "Where are the Jobs?: Searching for Job Openings," you can send a cover letter to a list of employers for which you would like to work to ask about job openings. The following is a sample of such a cover letter.

Sample Cover Letter – Cold Letter

HEATHER L. PARKS
1200 Music Street
Atlanta, Georgia 30303
(404) 111-1111
hp123@fakemailaddress.com

February 2, 2009

Mr. Walter Coleman
Hiring Partner
ABC Law Firm
1234 Symphony Way
Atlanta, GA 30309

Re: Associate Position in the Corporate Department at ABC Law Firm

Mr. Coleman:

I am writing to express my interest in any open associate positions at ABC Law Firm in the Corporate Department of your Atlanta, Georgia office. My current position is at Big Law Firm as an associate in the Corporate Department in Atlanta, Georgia. Prior to that, I worked in the Washington, DC office of Big Law Firm in the Corporate Department. As an attorney who practiced law in the District of Columbia for two years, and in Atlanta, Georgia, I have gained experience that will allow me to make a substantial contribution to ABC Law Firm.

At Big Law Firm, in addition to drafting and negotiating various merger agreements and associated documents, I recently closed the acquisition by my firm's client, a large national bank, of another bank. Additionally, I assisted in various aspects of the formation of state-chartered banks in Georgia. From the first day that I sat in my *Securities Regulation* course at Georgetown University Law Center to the Form 10-K I filed last week, I have enjoyed learning the intricacies of securities law and using that knowledge in my law practice. I would welcome the opportunity to join ABC Law Firm as an associate in the Corporate Department in Atlanta, Georgia where I can provide top-notch service to clients while working on sophisticated corporate matters only handled by a law firm such as your law firm.

Please find attached my resume. I would welcome the opportunity to meet with you. If you would like to meet with me, have any questions, or would like further information from me, please contact me at (404) 111-1111 or at home via e-mail at hp123@fakemailaddress.com. I look forward to hearing from you. Thank you for your consideration.

Sincerely,

Heather L. Parks

Attachment

26

Chapter Six

Who am I?
Your Resume

Your resume tells the employer who you are—at least career wise. Ideally, you should keep your resume to one page. Employers often receive several resumes. If your resume is unnecessarily too long, the employer might lose interest just because she is reading 200 resumes and reading three pages for one person is too much. If, however, you have been working for several years, or you have relevant information to the position for which you are applying that will not fit in one page, two pages is acceptable. If your resume is two pages, place your name and the page number in the top right-hand corner of the second page of your resume. Make sure that your resume is neat, there are no typos, there are no spelling mistakes, and the font is not too small (11 or 12 point font is a good size). The legal field is conservative so choose a font such as Times New Roman.

If you just graduated from law school, you can place your "Education" section first on your resume. If you have been out of law school for a few years and have relevant work experience, place your work experience first. Make sure that there are no gaps in employment on your resume. If there are gaps, be able to explain the gaps. In some instances, you might want to explain the gaps in your cover letter. For each job that you list on your resume, briefly describe relevant job tasks performed at each job. Make sure your resume is tailored to the position sought. For example, if while working at a law firm you worked in litigation as an associate and you were on the recruiting committee, if you are applying for an associate position, include more of the tasks associated with being an associate (e.g., drafted motions, drafted briefs). If you are applying for recruiting manager, include more of the tasks associated with being on the recruiting committee (e.g., screened several resumes after conducting interviews for associate positions in the law firm).

It is a good idea to keep a list of the matters that you are working on. After you finish a project, make it a habit of adding the project with the name of the client and a general description of the matter to the list. Not only can this help you when you are drafting or updating your resume but also with any conflicts checks that you may be required to complete prior to beginning your new job. Some employers will require a list of clients and matters prior to you beginning work for such a conflicts check. Although your list will include client names, do not include client names on your resume. See the chapter in this book entitled "Offer and Acceptance/Rejection" for more about pre-employment conflicts checks.

Should you include your GPA? If you have recently graduated from law school, your GPA might be of more interest to an employer than later in your career; however, some entities, such as large law firms, might be interested in your GPA at any point in your career. In general, if your GPA is good, include it. If it is not, do not include it.

But, realize that if you do not include your GPA, some individuals might assume that it is not good. If you include a GPA that is not so good, you can explain in your cover letter. For example, if the job opening asks for your GPA, provide your GPA even if your GPA is not a good one. If your GPA is not very good, explain in your cover letter what happened. If your first year was difficult as you adjusted to law school and your GPA was low, explain that but show how you improved your grades if that is what happened. An example could be: "My GPA is 2.9 because in my first semester of the first year of law school I had a low GPA, but after devising a plan to better my grades, my GPA in my last two years of law school was 3.5 or greater."

What is a good GPA? Like most things in life—it depends. If you went to a higher ranked law school, or one the employer considers to be a "good law school," an employer might accept your having a lower GPA than if you had the same GPA at a lower ranked school.[3] It is not fair, but it is a reality. Some employers will not care where you went to school, if you do not meet their threshold of a minimum GPA, you will not be considered as a viable candidate. Contact the career services office of your law school for a gauge of what is considered a "good GPA." Also, look at job openings for the places for which you would like to work to get an idea of what GPA is required or expected. I have always felt that even if your GPA does not meet the minimum criteria, as long as your GPA is not that far from the minimum, apply for the job anyway, especially if you can point to other skills or accomplishments that could be beneficial for the position sought.

This should not have to be said but DO NOT LIE ON YOUR RESUME. No explanation is needed—do not do it! Do not include the names of clients in the description of your work. Do not include your age, religious affiliations, political

---

[3] By "ranked," I am referring to the *U.S. News & World Report* which ranks law schools each year.

affiliations, or marital status unless you want to do this, or it is related to the job applied for (e.g., you are applying for a job as a blogger for Democrats and you are a Democrat) because not only is it not necessary but, unfortunately, for some employers, it might limit your job possibilities. Even though such behavior by employers can be illegal (e.g., not hiring a person because of his or her age can violate discrimination laws), that does not mean it won't still happen.

You may include other activities in which you are involved such as volunteer activities, or community activities, or even hobbies, but if there is no room on your resume, consider whether these items should be included. Sometimes these items are helpful to your job search. For example, if you want to work for a public interest organization that helps abused women, you want to show your interest in the area. Public interest employers, sometimes even more than other employers, want you to demonstrate your interest in the type of work the public interest organization does. Therefore, the fact that you volunteered at a women's shelter in law school would be something you would want to include. If you are a marathon runner, this could also be a helpful addition to your resume—it shows that you are hardworking and can "go the distance." I know, sorry, that was bad, but I couldn't resist.

If you worked on a temporary or contract basis, and you worked through an agency, list the agency as your employer, not the place where you were placed to do the work. I would not even mention the name of the entity where you were placed unless you receive permission to do so from that entity. Even then, do not list that entity as your employer. If you worked on a contract or temporary basis directly and not through an agency, you can put the place where you worked on a contract basis, but make sure to indicate that your work was on a contract basis. If you include your temporary or contract work on your resume, place either type of entry in the "Experience" section of your resume in chronological order. For examples of entries for temporary or contract work on your resume, see the end of this chapter.

For a sample resume, please see the end of this chapter. This is just one form of resume. Place your resume on the same high quality paper on which you placed your cover letter.

The application process for a job can differ depending on the target industry within law (e.g., government versus private sector versus public interest sector versus public defender/district attorney versus academia). For example, government applications can differ from applying to a law firm because often government positions require detailed applications, including a statement about your Knowledge, Skills and Abilities (KSAs), not just a resume and cover letter. For a good resource for those seeking legal jobs in the federal government, see the *2008-2009 Federal Legal Employment Opportunities Guide* at www.pslawnet.org/uploads/2008-2009_FLEOG_FINAL_PDF.pdf. For a good resource about KSAs, see www.doleta.gov/jobs/Federal_Application_ Process/Knowledge_ Skills_Abilities/. Do not worry about the different requirements for applying for certain jobs in the legal industry. The information about how to apply for the job, such as the information found in the job advertisement, should let you know what is expected.

Academia is another area where the application process and even the search process can be quite different. There are three general categories for attorneys that want to work at a law school—law professor, administrator, or adjunct professor. A resume for a professor position might be referred to as a curriculum vitae and can differ in form and substance. For example, there might be more emphasis on your publications in a curriculum vitae than on the usual resume. While some law professor jobs are posted on Web sites, many are not. One place that new professors are hired is at the Association of American Law Schools' Faculty Recruitment Conference. The Association of American Law Schools (AALS) holds this conference annually in Washington, DC in the fall where various schools and various candidates meet for interviews for professor positions. This book is not the place to thoroughly discuss the academic job search, but *please see Appendix I for helpful resources that discuss this topic further*.

A writing sample is another possible part of an application. Employers might ask you to submit a writing sample in addition to a resume. It is a good idea to have a writing sample prepared if you are thinking about searching for a job. However, while some employers will ask in general for a writing sample, some will be more specific (e.g., include a writing sample, not edited by others, that is no more than 10 pages). Make sure to follow instructions and submit a writing sample that complies with what is asked for.

Sample Resume

HEATHER L. PARKS
1200 Music Street
Atlanta, Georgia 30303
(404) 111-1111
hp123@fakemailaddress.com

EDUCATION

Georgetown University Law Center, Washington, DC
Juris Doctor, May 2005
The Georgetown Law Journal, Senior Articles Editor, 2004-2005; Staff, 2003-2004
Corporate Law Association

Rhodes College, Memphis, TN
Bachelor of Arts, History, magna cum laude, May 2002
Phi Beta Kappa
Dean's List (Every Semester)
Rhodes College Singers

EXPERIENCE

BIG LAW FIRM, Atlanta, GA
Associate, August 2007 – Present

Draft and negotiate merger agreements and associated documents. Manage and close mergers and acquisitions of banks. Assist in various aspects of the formation of state-chartered banks. Draft and file SEC filings such as the annual report on Form 10-K.

BIG LAW FIRM, Washington, DC
Associate, August 2005 – July 2007

Drafted memoranda concerning incorporation in Virginia and Maryland. Reviewed documents in relation to the sale of assets of a corporation. Drafted closing documents for mergers. Conducted research about blue sky laws in various states.

U.S. SECURITIES AND EXCHANGE COMMISSION, Washington, DC
Summer Honors Law Program, June – August 2004

Worked with SEC attorneys on various projects. Participated in seminars and workshops on aspects of federal securities laws such as securities fraud on the Internet. Took part in meetings that provided exposure to individuals and institutions in the securities and commodities industries and the legal profession.

SMALL LAW FIRM, Washington, DC
Summer Associate, May – August 2003

Researched and wrote legal memoranda concerning issues such as the required state filings for a bank established in Virginia. Assisted in drafting incorporation documents for a Maryland corporation.

Erin C. Coleman, JD

BAR ADMISSIONS

District of Columbia Bar (2005); State Bar of Georgia (2007)

PROFESSIONAL MEMBERSHIPS/OTHER ACTIVITIES (Past and Present)

American Bar Association, Women's Bar Association of the District of Columbia, GAWL (Georgia Association for Women Lawyers), Everybody Wins! Atlanta volunteer, Small Business Clinic volunteer

Sample Entries for Temporary or Contract Work

Contract Work Through an Agency

TEMP AGENCY, INC., Washington, DC
Contract Attorney, August 2005 – March 2006

Reviewed documents for responsiveness to a subpoena and for privilege in an FTC investigation. Supervised thirty other document reviewers (one of three individuals chosen to supervise document reviewers).

Contract Work Directly to a Law Firm

BIG LAW FIRM, Atlanta, GA
Contract Attorney, August 2005 – March 2006

Reviewed documents for responsiveness to a subpoena and for privilege in an FTC investigation. Supervised thirty other document reviewers (one of three individuals chosen to supervise document reviewers).

Chapter Seven

Pick Up—It's Your Future Calling

So, you have sent out your cover letters and resumes to employers, and now all you have to do is wait for them all to contact you to set up interviews—right? Wrong. Use this time to prepare for a possible interview. Although you might not be able to prepare everything because you do not know who is going to call you for an interview, there are some general things that you can work on even now to prepare for an interview. For example, you can make sure that your resume is in good shape so that when you take copies of your resume to the interview they will be in the best shape possible.[4] You can contact individuals to be your references, prepare the references document, and even go ahead and print out the copies that you will take to an interview with you.

You can also prepare for the call to ask you to come interview. Make sure that the telephone for the contact number that you placed in your cover letter or resume is functional. Don't laugh. For example, do not let the cell phone battery go dead so that you miss the call for the interview. Similarly, make sure that your e-mail address is functional. Make sure that your voicemail message is professional. If you do not regularly check voicemail and e-mails, do so while you are waiting to hear from potential employers.

---

[4] If you have updated or substantially changed your resume, and you distribute it to anyone at your interview, let people know that this is an updated resume.

Make sure that you are ready to speak to the person calling you to arrange an interview. For example, make sure that you have pen and paper readily accessible in the event that you get a call for an interview. If you do not, let the call go to voicemail and contact the person that contacted you about an interview immediately. You do not want to have to contact this person again to obtain information already given to you because you were unable to write the information down. It could leave a bad impression that you are not organized, for example. Also, do not answer your cell phone if you are on the subway or any other place where the cell phone reception could be intermittent or any other interruptions could distract you. Although you should not bother your contact for information that you have already been given, it is not the end of the world if you need to do so. It is better to have the correct information than to save face and arrive at the wrong place or at the wrong time for the interview. That will leave a worse impression than having to contact the person for information already given to you.

If you are contacted for an interview, make a list of any relevant information you will need to arrive at the interview on time and prepared. Such information includes, but is not limited to, the location and address of where you will be interviewing, the time of the interview, the person you should ask for when you arrive, and any materials you need to bring to the interview. Let the person contacting you offer this information, and if any item on your list of need to know items is not covered, ask for the information. If you are not clear about something, you can restate the information to make sure that you have all the correct information, or ask directly for any missing or unclear information.

Chapter Eight

Interview

Practice, Practice, Practice

Even if you are an expert at interviewing, practice before your interview. How much you practice will depend on how comfortable and experienced you are at interviewing. If you feel very comfortable interviewing, you probably do not need to actually participate in a mock interview. However, make sure that you know your resume backwards and forwards and that you know and remember the details about every item listed on your resume. For example, if you have the note you wrote in law school listed on your resume, pull it out and scan it before your interview, so that if asked, you can intelligently discuss your note.

Also, think about interview questions you might be asked and how you would answer the questions. Know the answers well enough so that the answers do not seem rehearsed. Your answers should be how you truly feel. Be honest in answering questions. If you lie (which you should not do in an interview anyway) or give answers that you think are correct, the answers might sound fake. However, proceed with caution—if you hated your boss, do not use your interview as the vehicle to vent about your boss. Answer the questions, but, do not dwell on the negative. For example, if your grades in law school were not good and you are asked about your grades, acknowledge that your grades were not what you wanted, but, if your grades improved, talk more about how you took a challenging situation, devised a plan, followed the plan, and increased your grades. Focus more on your overcoming a challenge instead of the bad grades. *For a list of questions that you might be asked in an interview, see Appendix G.*

If you need more practice interviewing, ask a friend to conduct a mock interview. If your law school career services office offers the service, arrange an appointment with a career counselor specifically for a mock interview. While it is best to do this in person, if your law school is in another city, do the mock interview over the phone. A mock interview can especially be helpful for atypical interviews such as those conducted by a district attorney's office or a public defender's office. For example, an interview for a public defender's office can include questions that give you a hypothetical situation based on events that could and do happen at trial and that ask how you would handle such. Let the person who will be giving you the mock interview know what type of interview for which you need practice. The career services offices should be able to tailor your mock interview accordingly or provide you with reading materials to prepare for an atypical interview.

For the actual job interview, take copies of your resume with you. Also, prepare questions for the individual or individuals who will be interviewing you. This is your opportunity to ask questions that are important to you. Do not ask questions for which the answers are easily obtained, for example, on the employer's Web site. Have several questions— you might get an interviewer who is either busy or not very good at interviewing and a thirty minute interview might consist of five minutes of the interviewer speaking with his last question being, "Well, do you have any questions for me?," with him giving you one or two word answers to your questions. *For a list of possible interview questions that you can ask, see Appendix G.*

What Not to Wear...To Your Interview

Although many employers have embraced business casual attire, the legal profession is still pretty conservative when it comes to dress. Even if you will never have to wear a suit again if hired, wear a suit to your interview. Men should wear a dark suit, such as blue or gray with a tie and a light colored shirt, preferably white. Women should wear a suit, or dress and jacket, in a dark color such as blue, black, or gray and should wear pantyhose. Both men and women should wear closed toed, dress shoes that are in good condition and preferably shined. Wear little jewelry. For example, women should wear small earrings such as pearls, or diamond studs, or very small hoop earrings, or something similar to these items. Do not wear perfume or cologne. Do not add anything to your wardrobe that will draw unnecessary attention to you or distract the interviewer. Make sure that your nails are clean and that you are well-groomed—that your hair is combed, cut if needed. If it is raining, be prepared—carry an umbrella and a raincoat so that your interview look will not be ruined. Women, carry an extra pair of pantyhose in your purse in the event that the pair that you are wearing become torn. Women, do not wear a lot of makeup—subtlety is best. Your interview is not the time to try something new, so if you were always dreaming about getting a Mohawk hairstyle—wait until after you have completed interviewing. Women, carry a small purse. If you live in a commuter city, you can carry a very nice tote or briefcase to carry your commuter gear (i.e., snow boots, scarf).

Follow the Yellow Brick Road…or MapQuest…or Whatever Will Help You to Arrive at the Correct Interview Place On Time

Make sure that you know where you are going for your interview. Some employers have more than one office in the same city. If you have not received information already about your interview day, confirm before your interview where you are supposed to be and when you are supposed to be there. If you need to confirm interview day information, it is a good idea to ask your contact at the employer who is providing information about the logistics of your interview via e-mail so that you will have the correct information in writing. Ask this person also for directions using the mode of transportation you will be using. If you are using a commuter train, tell the person. For example, ask: "What is the best way to get to your office using the Metro coming from Arlington?" Leave early so that you will arrive at your interview 10 to 15 minutes prior to your scheduled time. If the city is known for traffic or the train system is prone to break down, leave even earlier. Even if you arrive at the office building earlier than 10 or 15 minutes prior to your interview, and you do not want to go in too early, make sure that you are in the right place and go to the coffee shop next door or somewhere nearby, if necessary.

Act Like You Have "Home Training" Even if You Do Not

Unfortunately, some in society, and in the legal profession, feel entitled and, therefore, act in such a manner. You should arrive at any place and say "Hello" to people and treat them with respect, but, if you do not believe in common courtesy, or do not exercise good "home training," or think that everyone in the world was born to serve you, when you arrive at your hopefully future employer's place of business, realize that often the decision makers about whether you will be hired are not only on the recruiting committee. If you are unpleasant to the receptionist or the secretary for the individual with whom you will be interviewing, this can harm your chances. Sometimes, people making hiring decisions will ask others in their office what he or she thought of the candidate. You want the person to be able to say that you were polite and professional at the very least. Also, remember, if you get the job, these will be your coworkers. You do not want to start off on the wrong foot.

When you are waiting to go in for your interview, assume that you are being watched by anyone else in the room, because you are being watched. Do not talk on your cell phone. In fact, you should have turned your phone off unless you need to keep the phone on silent for a possible important call. It is up to you what is an important call. Once you are invited back to begin your interview, shake the person's hand firmly, look the person in the eye, and wait to be asked to take a seat. If the person never offers a seat, ask "May I have a seat?"

Attitude is Everything

This might sound hokey, but positive thinking will help you in your job search and, in particular, at your interview. If you do not think that you can get the job, no one else will. This is not just about cosmic feelings and karma, but there is a practical reason that this is true. If you do not think you will get the job or deserve the job, this will show in your demeanor and how you answer questions in your interview. More than likely, you will carry yourself in a manner that is negative and low in confidence and with little enthusiasm. Part of your job in an interview is to convince the employer that you are the person for the job. If you haven't even convinced yourself, how will you convince anyone else?

Chapter Nine

References

Do not include your references on your resume—do not place "References Available Upon Request" on your resume. Instead, include the names and contact information of your references on a separate piece of paper. Place your name on the piece of paper in the top, right-hand corner. Before listing a person as a reference, ask his or her permission and let the person know for what position you are listing him or her as a reference. If you are using the person for several positions for which you are applying, you can let him or her know in general what type of jobs for which you are applying instead of describing each job. For example, "law firm associate positions" would suffice. Make sure that you provide references that meet the criteria asked for if the job opening asks for a specific reference. For example, if the job opening asks for a reference from someone who has been your direct supervisor, do not ask your fellow associates to be references.

A good reference is more than just someone who will speak favorably about you and your work. A good reference has worked with you enough to know your work and speak about you and your work. A bad reference could be someone who speaks highly of you but cannot really speak to your work.

Ask your references to be discreet and to not let anyone else know about your job search if your job search is a secret. It is possible that the job for which you are applying asks for a reference from your current employer. Choose wisely. If at all possible, choose someone who can keep your job search a secret while still providing you a good reference.

For an example of how to prepare your references, see the next page. Place your references on the same high quality paper on which you placed your cover letter and resume. Keep your references with you when you go to your interview. You might be asked for your references at the interview.

Sample References

Heather L. Parks

REFERENCES

Bob Jones, Partner
Big Law Firm
2130 13th Street NW
Washington, DC 20005
(202) 123-4567

Julia Jackson, Partner
Big Law Firm
1455 Peach Street
Atlanta, Georgia 30303
(404) 765-4321

Meredith Smith, Executive Director
Small Business Clinic
5678 Georgia Avenue NW
Washington, DC 20010
(202) 999-0000

Chapter Ten

Thank You

After your interview, send a thank you note to the person or persons who interviewed you. The thank you letter does not have to be long and can be either handwritten or typed. Try to mention something that you want the interviewer to remember or something you discussed, such as an article. You can either mail your thank you letter or send an e-mail. Personally, I like to send a typed thank you letter and mail the letter. I think it is more professional; however, e-mail thank you letters are acceptable. The benefit of e-mailing your thank you letter is that it will be received more quickly than if placed in the mail. If you use mail, mail your thank you letter no later than the next day after your interview. Whatever method you use, make sure that you send your thank you letter within twenty-four hours of your interview. A compromise between the mailing method and the e-mail method is to e-mail the letter you would otherwise send through the mail as an attachment instead of placing the thank you in the body of an e-mail.

If you met with several people for your interview, send a thank you letter to each person with whom you interviewed. Make sure to not send the exact same thank you letter to each person. You can use the same form but tailor each letter for the conversation you had with each person. If you met with too many people to send a thank you to each person (e.g., 20 people), send your thank you letter to the Hiring Partner, or Recruiting Director, or contact person who coordinated your interviews and ask him or her to forward it to others.

For an example of a thank you letter, please see the next page. If mailed, place your thank you letter on the same high quality paper on which you placed your cover letter, resume, and references.

Sample Thank You Letter

HEATHER L. PARKS
1200 Music Street
Atlanta, Georgia 30303
(404) 111-1111
hp123@fakemailaddress.com

March 2, 2009

Mr. Walter Coleman
Hiring Partner
ABC Law Firm
1234 Symphony Way
Atlanta, GA 30309

Dear Mr. Coleman:

Thank you for allowing me to interview at ABC Law Firm. I enjoyed meeting you, and I appreciated the opportunity to speak with you and to learn more about the Corporate Department as well as the position for which I am interviewing. If you have any further questions of me, please feel free to contact me at (404) 111-1111 or at home via e-mail at hp123@fakemailaddress.com. I look forward to hearing from you.

Sincerely,

Heather L. Parks

Chapter Eleven

Follow-up

So you have done everything you can—you have created a great resume and cover letter, you applied for the position of your dreams, you had what you think is a great interview, and promptly sent a thank you note. Now you wait for the phone to ring. Not exactly. You should not wait forever for the phone to ring for two reasons. One—some employers might not call you to tell you that you did not get the job. Two—you can contact the employer to determine your status if you do not hear from the employer with whom you interviewed. The key is to make sure that you adhere to what the employer wants about follow-up. Try to establish these parameters before you leave from your interview. Hopefully, the employer will say to you that he or she will be in contact with you by a certain date or in a certain amount of time, but that does not always happen. If the employer does not say anything about when you can expect to hear from her, you can politely ask when does she think that you might be able to hear from her. This can be tricky because the employer might not like the question and might feel pressured. If you do not want to take this risk, you can choose not to ask the question.

If you have been given a time frame of when you should expect to hear from the employer, try to adhere to that and do not contact the employer before the time frame has expired. For example, if the employer says that he or she expects to contact you in two weeks with a decision, do not call the next day asking about whether the employer has made a decision. If the given time frame has expired, or if you were never given a time frame and it has been some time since your interview, unless the employer said "no phone calls please," you can contact either the person with whom you interviewed, or your contact (e.g., the recruiting manager in a law firm), or whoever you were told to call with questions. Preferably, contact a person who will know where the employer is in the interview process as far as you are concerned.

If you do contact someone after your interview, do not be rude or demanding. The following is a possible script to use: "My name is Heather Parks. I interviewed with your firm on March 2, 2009. I do not want to be a bother, but I am very interested in the position for which I interviewed and was wondering where your firm is in the decision making process." Employers should not be upset with this phone call. You should get some indication of where the process stands and hopefully a date by which you will be contacted. But, realize, the decision making process can take a long time depending on the employer for which you interviewed. For example, if you interviewed in a law firm and met with several people, all of their evaluations have to be collected, and more than likely the firm recruiting committee has to meet. If you interviewed with federal or even local government, the decision making process can take even longer.

Even though some follow-up is okay, do not become a pest. If the employer has said in your follow-up call that he will contact you with a decision by June 1st, do not call again before June 1st. In the end, you will have to decide based on your personality and comfort level how much follow-up you will engage in.

If after your following up, you don't hear from an employer with whom you interviewed, move on as if you have not gotten the job. In fact, while in the job search process, do not stop going on interviews after having an interview even if you think your interview went really well. Do not stop searching for a job or going on interviews until you have accepted a job.

Chapter Twelve

Salary

Know what you can afford and be realistic. If you need a job to pay your bills, you might not have as much leeway to turn down a job, but determining the salary that is right for you is more than whether you can pay your bills. Ask yourself whether you will be able to sustain your lifestyle with this salary. Although it is true that having work that makes you truly happy is important, if you are not making enough money to live in a manner where you are not worried about money or where you cannot enjoy the lifestyle you wish, you might end up resenting taking the job. I once thought that I had my dream job and very willingly took a pay cut to have this job, but the dream became a nightmare when I realized that the job, although a good and somewhat enjoyable job, was not the dream that I thought it was, especially given the fact that I was making only enough to barely pay my bills.

For those of you whose job search is not in the near future, you can plan for switching jobs. If you plan to take a pay cut, start living a lifestyle for the salary you will be making instead of your current salary. Save your money. It is not a bad idea to save your money even if you are not searching for a job. You never know when you might need to make a job change quickly. For example, your spouse is moving, you have taken the last screaming fit from your boss, or the job of your dreams lands on your desk. Having money saved can give you the flexibility to make a job change and especially make a job change quickly if necessary.

Remember that salary alone is not always the only part of the package. You should also investigate the benefits given with the job. You should have already thought about what benefits you need at this stage in your life. Depending on what is important to you, certain benefits might make up for a not so stellar salary. For example, maybe the future employer matches contributions to your 401(k) at a higher rate than your prior job. If that is important to you, a pay cut might not be so bad given the benefits.

There are many resources for finding out about salaries for a particular position. One of the first places to start is job ads. Sometimes the job ads, especially for government positions, will list the salary (e.g., www.usajobs.opm.gov/). Some Web sites that provide salary information are:

www.salary.com

www.cbsalary.com

www.infirmation.com/shared/insider/payscale.tcl (This Web site contains information that is not current. For example, there are salaries listed as far back as 2003.)

www.nalpdirectory.com

NALP is an association for legal career professionals such as career services professionals, recruitment professionals, and professional development professionals. NALP provides information about salaries in the legal profession. For example, if you are interested in private firm salaries, the annual *Associate Salary Survey* provided by NALP can be useful. You can purchase this from the NALP bookstore or even better, you can contact your career services office in your law school. More than likely, it will have a current copy of the guide and can provide you salary information.

Another source, for those interested in public interest and public sector positions, is the *Public Sector & Public Interest Attorney Salary Report*. This also can be purchased at the NALP bookstore, but, again, contact career services to see its copy if so purchased, or see if someone in the office can give you the information that you need from the report.

Another source for information about legal employers is the *NALP Directory of Legal Employers* (www.nalpdirectory .com/). This directory is based on information submitted by the employers themselves. Choose "Advanced Search" and you can choose by different criteria such as "Employer Type" or "City." For example, you can choose "Corporate," "Government," "Law Firm," or "Public Interest" to get a list of employers. Click on the name of the employer to obtain salary and benefit information.

Positions in the federal government are often on a grade level with a corresponding salary range. Many of the advertisements for federal government positions will give you this grade level and salary range for the job. For jobs in the federal government, see www.usajobs.opm.gov/. A good resource about the grade levels in the federal government is the *Federal Legal Employment Opportunities Guide*. The most recent version of this can be found at www.pslawnet.org/uploads/2008-2009_FLEOG_FINAL_PDF .pdf.

If you are interested in recruiting and career services positions, Eva Wisnik, President of Wisnik Career Enterprises, Inc., conducted a survey of legal recruitment professionals in various cities. At least one survey also included law school career services professionals. (See the survey for Washington, DC for 2008.) To view these salary surveys for recruiting professionals in locations such as Atlanta, Georgia, Washington, DC, New York, New York, Houston, Texas, and the Bay Area, see www.wisnik.com/. (Choose "Jobs For Recruiters." Then choose "Salary Survey.")

Last, but not least, contact your law school's career services office. The individuals in that office will know about salary information in your geographic area and more than likely will have various resources with salary information.

Some of the resources that provide salary information are more reliable than others. For example, some of the Internet sites that compile information by asking the viewers of its Web sites to provide salary information may or may not have accurate information.

If you are asked to provide your salary requirements in a cover letter or in the interview, you can say that "salary is negotiable." If you are pressed, give a figure based on your research of the market for the salary for the job (e.g., industry, geography), but try to avoid this question if at all possible. If you give a salary that is too high, you can price yourself out of a job. If you give a salary that is too low, you could miss out on making more money.

Should you ask about salary in an interview? A general rule is to not bring up salary and compensation until you receive an offer and to not be the first to bring up the salary figure.[5] I agree. Again, if you give a salary that is too high, you can price yourself out of a job. If you give a salary that is too low, you could miss out on making more money.

For good books that discuss salary negotiation, see *What Color Is Your Parachute? 2006: A Practical Manual for Job-Hunters and Career-Changers* by Richard Nelson Bolles (starting at page 313[6]) and *Women & Money: Owning the Power to Control Your Destiny* by Suze Orman (starting at page 31). Although the focus of *Women & Money* is women, the discussion about salary, worth, and asking for what one is worth can be helpful to women and men.

---

[5] See Marcia Bench, *Career Coaching: An Insider's Guide* (Mountain View, CA: Davies-Black Publishing, 2003), 281. Note that a second edition of this book has been written—*Career Coaching: An Insider's Guide-Second Edition* by Marcia A. Bench. See also Richard Nelson Bolles, *What Color Is Your Parachute? 2006: A Practical Manual for Job-Hunters and Career-Changers*, 2006 ed. (Berkeley, CA: Ten Speed Press, 2006), 314-315. This book is revised each year and there is a 2009 edition.
[6] This book is revised each year and there is a 2009 edition.

Chapter Thirteen

Offer and Acceptance/Rejection

You get a call. Good news, you have been offered the job! In a best case scenario, you would have thought about whether you would accept the job if offered. You should think about this with the only reason for needing a lot of time to decide whether to accept is if the offer is substantially different from what you thought it would be. If you have thought about whether you would accept this job if offered, and all of the terms meet with your approval, you could accept the job when offered. However, even in this situation, I would wait at least an hour to think things through before accepting the offer. On the other hand, do not wait too long to accept if you know this is the job and terms you want. There is no need to wait a week to accept in this situation. You could run the risk of the job offer being rescinded. If you truly need time to think about a job offer, take some time. For example, if the salary is much less than you thought, and you really need time, take some time, but stay in contact with the person that offered you the job and work out a time frame with this person to get back to him that meets his criteria as well as yours. For example, let the employer know that you are interested, but that this is a big decision, and ask if you could have more time to think about the offer. Do not extend the time too long. Again, you run the risk of the offer being rescinded.

You interview for two positions—an "Okay Job" and your "Dream Job." What if you get an offer for the "Okay Job" before your "Dream Job"? That depends on your ultimate goal. There is no right or wrong answer. If you do not have a job and you need a job sooner rather than later, you might need to take the "Okay Job." This will also depend on when you must accept or decline the offer. If you have a present job and can live with the possibility of staying in that job, it might be best for you to reject the "Okay Job" in hopes of getting an offer for the "Dream Job." But, realize that you might not get an offer for the "Dream Job" and will have to stay where you are. If that is okay with you, this strategy works.

Whatever your circumstances, remain professional. If you have agreed to give an answer to an offer in a set amount of time, adhere to that. For example, if you agree to provide an answer in one week, do so, or call within the one week time and ask for an extension. You could say that you need the time because this is a big decision.

If you know you do not want a job, reject the offer tactfully and quickly. Don't keep people hanging needlessly. Make sure to thank them for their time and the offer. The employer still might feel you wasted her time because you interviewed for a position that you are now rejecting but that cannot be helped. You might be asked what is your reason for rejecting the offer. You can be general in your answer to this question. For example: "Thank you, but I have decided to pursue other opportunities," or if you would like, you can be more specific about your reasons for rejecting the offer, but I recommend being honest with as few details as possible. No matter what, have a good reason.

Get things in writing as much as possible, such as the offer with the particular position named, salary, benefits, start date, and any other information that is important to you. Once you have an offer, contact the person to whom you are to give your answer and accept or reject the offer over the phone. Although it is not usually necessary to accept a job offer in writing, you could also send an acceptance letter accepting the offer and acknowledging the offer letter if you received such a letter in addition to accepting over the phone. You might state in your acceptance letter: "I accept your offer of employment as an associate in the Corporate Department of ABC Law Firm as described in your offer letter dated April 1, 2009." If you have negotiated something different from the offer letter, state the new terms in your acceptance letter. The sentence might change as follows: "I accept your offer of employment as an associate in the Corporate Department of ABC Law Firm as described in your offer letter dated April 1, 2009, said letter having been amended by our conversation on April 2nd concerning salary which is now $200,000 per year." It is even better if the firm sends you a new offer letter with the new terms (e.g., salary) described therein. For books that discuss negotiating an offer, see *Career Coaching: An Insider's Guide* by Marcia Bench starting at page 279[7] and *What Color Is Your Parachute? 2006: A Practical Manual for Job-Hunters and Career-Changers* by Richard Nelson Bolles starting at page 313[8].

As suggested earlier in this book, keep a list of clients and matters on which you have worked while you are working on them. If you go from one law firm to another, more than likely, you will have to submit a conflicts report—a list of the clients for which you have worked and the name and description of the matter—for a period of time. You may be

---

[7] A second edition of *Career Coaching: An Insider's Guide* has been written—*Career Coaching: An Insider's Guide-Second Edition* by Marcia A. Bench.

[8] This book is revised each year and there is a 2009 edition.

required to present even more information such as opposing party names or opposing law firms. Remember, if any of this information is confidential or privileged, adhere to that, and do not divulge anything in your conflicts report that would break the privilege or confidentiality. Work with your new firm for a solution that will protect privilege and confidentiality and meet the criteria of its conflicts checks. Some firms will not allow you to start with the law firm until this list has been reviewed and cleared by them. The object is to avoid any conflicts of interests by your new employment. Gathering this information and remembering this information can be a time-consuming process and might hold up your ability to start the new job.

The advice given in this book is often general and is a starting place, but, specific instructions from the employer to whom you are applying, about a particular situation, will often trump this general advice. For example, although there is a chapter in this book about how one can handle accepting a position, an employer might require that you sign a form, provided by the employer, that memorializes the offer and your acceptance instead of you providing an acceptance letter. In that instance, you should sign the form to accept the offer instead of providing an acceptance letter.

If you have a current job, you will need to resign. Check your present employer's policy. This may be found in an employee handbook, for example. More than likely, the policy will not be mandatory. For example, a policy may state that "it is appropriate for associates to give four weeks notice when resigning." Of course, a statement such as this is not mandatory. You will need to determine what is best for you and your current employer. Remember, you want to leave your employer on good terms, even if it is the worst place to work and your coworkers are not being professional about your leaving. You be professional. Give yourself enough time to finish any projects, or at least get your work to a point where the person that must take over your work can easily do so.

You must also think of yourself and your future employer. When does your future employer need you to start? Were you going to take any time off in between jobs? All other things considered, two weeks notice is standard. In my experience, all other things considered as discussed herein, two weeks notice is a good choice.

For an example of an acceptance letter and a resignation letter, please see the next few pages.

Sample Acceptance Letter

April 2, 2009

Mr. Walter Coleman
Hiring Partner
ABC Law Firm
1234 Symphony Way
Atlanta, GA 30309

Dear Mr. Coleman:

I accept your offer of employment as an associate in the Corporate Department of ABC Law Firm, as described in your offer letter dated April 1, 2009, a copy of which is attached hereto, as amended by our conversation today concerning salary which is now $200,000 per year.

Thank you for your offer of employment, and I look forward to working for ABC Law Firm.

Sincerely,

Heather L. Parks

Sample Resignation Letter

April 3, 2009

Ms. Meredith L. Johnson
Managing Partner
Big Law Firm
1455 Peach Street
Atlanta, Georgia 30303

Dear Ms. Johnson:

This is to inform you of my resignation as an associate at Big Law Firm effective at the close of business on April 17, 2009 to accept employment at ABC Law Firm.

I wish to thank Big Law Firm for the opportunity to work at the law firm, and I wish the firm continued success.

Sincerely,

Heather L. Parks

Chapter Fourteen

It's Only Temporary
Contract Work

Why mention this topic in a job search book? Because, if you do not have a job, while you are searching for a job, this can be a stop gap measure to pay your bills until you get a job. Legal contract work is generally where you perform legal work for a set period of time (e.g., 3 months) and are paid by the hour. Unlike a salaried position, you are only paid when you work and for the amount of hours you work. The type of work can be anything from document review to taking the place of, and functioning as, an associate at a law firm.

There is some debate about whether contract work is a viable option, but for someone who has had good experiences with contract work, depending on your goals and circumstances, it can be a very viable option. If you are in between jobs and need to pay the bills, contract work can be a very good option. However, do not use contract work as the way to get a permanent job. That may or may not happen, but don't count on it. But, know that it does happen. Remember that even though the contract work is only a temporary position, treat it as if it was a permanent job and be a professional.

Just like any job can be a good experience or a bad experience, contract jobs can be a good experience or a bad experience. A good experience would be one in which the hiring entity treats you as if you are an employee of that entity (even though you are not) by, for example, giving you an office or a nice work station, including you in firm functions, and providing you with the tools you need to do the job well with reasonable hours. A bad experience would be one where you are one of thirty individuals in a basement room with no windows and a temperamental air and heating unit, you are working eleven-hour days, and reviewing accounting records where you have a quota of how many documents you must complete reviewing. Both ends of the spectrum occur. Do your homework. Find out how the hiring entity treats its contract workers. Ask your contract work agency recruiter. Ask other contract workers that you know. You might even search the Internet, but remember, this information might not be accurate.

You can contract your services through an agency or directly to the hiring entity. There are pros and cons to both of these methods. If you do it yourself, and contract with the entity directly, depending on how you structure your contract, if you are a true independent contractor, you are responsible for withholding your own taxes and paying the social security tax that an employer would usually pay. However, you might be able to negotiate a higher per hour rate if you contract with the entity directly. If you work through an agency, the agency places you on your assignment and determines your hourly rate.

If the agency places you at a firm, for example, the agency will be paid by the firm for your services and the agency will pay you. So, if you work forty hours per week, the firm might pay the agency $50.00 per hour for each of the forty hours you worked that week—$2,000.00. The agency might then pay you $30.00 per hour—$1,200.00. If you had worked for that firm directly, you might have been able to contract with the firm at $50.00 per hour instead of $30.00. But realize, agencies have information that you might not have about job openings, so, in the example above, you might not have even known about the job at the law firm. Also, some agencies offer benefits—something a firm probably would not offer you as a direct contractor (even though there are exceptions). Some agencies offer 401(k) benefits, health benefits, etcetera. But, get all of the details. Find out what are the criteria for keeping those benefits. For example, what happens when your contract job ends? Another benefit of an agency is that the agency will often be your employer, so that it will withhold taxes and do other things that a traditional employer would do such as pay social security tax; however, do your research—every agency is not the same.

Some say that doing contract work can hurt your career because future employers might think that you did contract work because you couldn't get a job elsewhere. However, some people choose to do contract work even if they could get a job elsewhere as an option to do other things such as write or act and because of the flexibility that contract work can offer. For a good book about contract work, see *The Complete Guide to Contract Lawyering: What Every Lawyer and Law Firm Needs to Know about Temporary Legal Services, 3rd Edition* by Deborah Arron and Deborah Guyol.

My personal opinion is whether or not contract work is a good option depends on your story—why you are doing contract work. If you need to pay your bills, contract work is better than no work—a good reason to do contract work. If you are making lifestyle choices or trying to pursue other things (new career, flexibility) doing contract work can facilitate those lifestyle choices—a good reason to do contract work. Some people prefer contract work because of the ability to choose short assignments and the flexibility it provides—a good reason to do contract work. Are you learning (good) or only doing the same type of work (not as good)? Are you doing document review only over several years (not as good), or are you a specialist that contracts your services (good)? Did you have to suddenly move to a new city (good)? Are you in the beginning of your career and all you have done is contract work and would like a more permanent job (not as good), or are you at the end of your career and want to transition out of the practice of law (good)? Even the "not so good" items can be good depending on your story. If you like document review, and you don't want to be a partner in a law firm, and you really want to be an actor, "not so good" becomes "good." If you are at the beginning of your career in a soft market and cannot get a job, "not so good" becomes "good."

Some people do not put contract work on their resumes. I disagree, especially if you did contract work for any length of time. You do not want gaps on your resume and as long as you can explain why you did the contract work, placing this information on your resume is fine.

For a list of agencies that provide contract work for lawyers, see Appendix K. I am not recommending one agency over another; however, I did have a good experience working with HIRECounsel in Washington, DC. Before joining one of these agencies, investigate the agency to determine if doing contract work through this agency is right for you. Ask people who have worked with the agency about their experiences. See if anyone has commented about the agency on the Internet. But, take any personal accounts either in person or on the Internet with a grain of salt, because a contract work experience can depend on the particular placement for the contract work (i.e., the firm where the person is placed) and the person. Each person can have a different experience with contract work.

Chapter Fifteen

What's the Alternative?
The Alternative Career Job Search

Some individuals will decide either the day after law school ends or ten years later that practicing law is not for them. If this describes you, you do not have to take your law degree off of the wall and pack it into a dark closet. There are many alternatives to practicing law and ways to use your law degree.

Many individuals with law degrees have gone on to pursue other careers—in and outside of law—that make them much happier and fulfilled than practicing law did—author, consultant, actor, coach (e.g., career coach or life coach), teacher—the list goes on and on. There are many jobs that require or prefer a JD: legal writing professor, professional development positions, law professor, legal career services positions in law schools, other administrative positions in law schools, and writers who write about legal topics. For examples and stories of individuals with law degrees who have succeeded at obtaining alternative careers, see www.jdblissblog.com. There is also a blog called JDSnub Blog (www.jdsnub. typepad.com) with posts about attorneys who have transitioned into positions other than practicing law.[9] And, for another Web site with information for lawyers in career transition and stories of lawyers who have successfully obtained alternative careers to

---

[9] Blogs can provide additional, helpful information concerning your career. Another interesting blog is Above the Law (www.abovethelaw.com). For the *ABA Journal*'s second annual list of the best legal blogs, see Molly McDonough and Sarah Randag, "The Blawg 100: Best of the Blogosphere," *ABA Journal*, December 2008, 34-43.

practicing law, see www.darlinghill.com/category/detours. *For a list of types of positions for those who want to be recovering lawyers (i.e., those with a law degree who do not practice law any more), and Web sites that list job openings for those positions, see Appendix J.* For a good book about leaving the corporate work environment, see *Escape from Corporate America: A Practical Guide to Creating the Career of Your Dreams* by Pamela Skillings. Although *Escape from Corporate America* discusses all corporate environments, not just law firms, this book provides helpful information for a person experiencing a career transition out of a corporate environment.

Even when conducting a job search for a position other than a lawyer position, many of the job search techniques used in this book can be used for non-lawyer positions. However, the farther you get away from the legal profession, the less likely it is that you can rely on this book which is primarily geared toward the legal profession. For example, the resume sample in this book could be used for obtaining a job as a career counselor in a law school but not for an actor. You could still rely on parts of the book, however, such as the advice in this book about networking or informational interviewing. That would be a great way to start to research what you will need to do in a non-legal job search.

If you attempt to obtain a position not practicing law as soon as you graduate, you might not have an easy time doing so, but it is not impossible. Many of these alternative legal positions list as one of the requirements of the position (or a preference for) some legal experience. If you have practiced for at least a short time, you will be able to bring that experience to one of these positions and might have an easier time transitioning into the position. If you do not have legal experience, or you are still in law school, follow some of the suggestions in the next paragraph anyway. Just modify them for your situation. For example, you can write law review articles if you want to teach law. You might not be able to be on a recruiting committee of a law firm, but, try to work or volunteer in career services at your law school.

Having legal experience and experience in the area into which you want to transition can be very valuable. If you know that you want to transition to the recruiting department of a law firm, get on the recruiting committee of the law firm while you are an associate. If you want to teach law, write an article, or several articles, that can be published in a law review. Volunteer in the area in which you want to work. Write articles about the area in which you want to transition. If you want to work in a certain legal subject area, join the section of the American Bar Association or your local bar association that is for that subject area. If you want to work in knowledge management, join the technology committee, or join your law firm section's initiative to create forms, or checklists, or a memorandum bank. If you want to be a writer, of course, write. Write in areas in which you might want to be a full-time writer. Get published whether in a firm newsletter, the editorial page of a newspaper, a law review, a legal publication, blog, or Web site. By doing these things, not only will you gain experience, you will show your commitment to transitioning to a new area. Also, if you decide to continue practicing law and become a partner, for example, none of these activities would be wasted time and would only help you to become a partner.

So, now that you know that you don't want to practice law, you have an idea of what you might want to do next, you have been doing things to help position you for this next career move such as writing articles and joining committees, now what? Now you need to find open positions. Job openings are listed everywhere. However, do not limit yourself to apply only to posted jobs. See the chapter in this book entitled "Where are the Jobs?: Searching for Job Openings." These places will often also contain alternative legal jobs as well. In addition to the places listed in the chapter entitled "Where are the Jobs?: Searching for Job Openings," the following paragraph includes some specific places on the Internet to find alternative legal jobs.

You can find alternative legal jobs on job Web sites such as monster.com, law.com, and craigslist.[10] NALP has compiled a list of Web sites for lawyers interested in alternative careers. See "Alternative Careers for Lawyers: Web Sites of Interest" prepared by NALP Alternative Careers Committee, Fall 2003 – Updated 2008 at www.nalp.org/assets/296_ alternativecareerswebsite.pdf. In addition to these general job search boards, certain alternative careers have Web sites with job postings specific to the area. For example, if you are interested in recruiting, professional development, or career services positions, see the Web site for NALP (www.nalp.org) for open positions.[11] If you are interested in teaching law, you can find positions at *The Chronicle of Higher Education* (chronicle.com). Although the more specific Web sites (e.g.,

---

[10] There is even a Web site dedicated to alternative jobs for lawyers— Alternative Lawyer Jobs. For a list of alternative job openings for lawyers, see www.alternativelawyerjobs.com. This Web site lists what I would consider truly alternative jobs for lawyers (e.g., legal writers for a legal research company), and jobs that I would characterize more as alternatives to practicing law in a firm more than a truly alternative job (e.g., general counsel position).

[11] Once at www.nalp.org, choose "Jobs."

chronicle.com) will list openings at law schools for teaching, career services, and other administrative positions, also look at school Web sites for openings. For example, a law school might list an opening in its career services office on its Web site instead of NALP since NALP charges a per month fee for listing a position on its Web site. For additional information concerning pursuing legal teaching positions and recruiting positions, see the chapter in this book entitled "Who Am I?: Your Resume." *See also Appendix I (Resources—Academic Job Search) for more information about the academic job search. For more Web sites associated with alternative careers, see Appendix J.*

Make sure that your resume and cover letter are tailored for the position for which you are applying. For example, if you want to work in recruiting at a law firm, emphasize that you have interviewed individuals for summer associate positions and that you have been on the recruiting committee for two years over the many Form 10-K filings that you have completed. Do not delete your legal experience—that can be important to alternative career positions as well—but highlight the skills needed for the job for which you are applying.

"But," you ask, "will I be able to pay my student loan bills?" One myth that exists out there is that if you are going to use your law degree and not practice law in a big firm, you will have to take such a pay cut that you will have to become best friends with Mr. Jif and Ms. Smucker's and eat peanut butter and jelly sandwiches every day. Although this diet might not be a problem for all of the three-year olds in our lives, most of us so called grown ups probably wouldn't last a month on this type of diet—and you don't have to. While it is true that in most cases you will need to take a pay cut for certain alternative legal positions, it might not be as big of a shearing as you think. For example, in a 2008 survey of legal recruiting and law school career services professionals in Washington, DC, the average salary for law firm directors was $156,556.[12] And, for all of those critics out there who will feel that this is ridiculous because given the economic times, and the fact that most people do not make six figures, and any person crying because they have to make $50,000 instead of $160,000 is a big cry baby, hear this. Law school is expensive, and the reality is that many of us have huge student loans to repay, or we might have children, or older parents, or other obligations that require a certain amount of money. Or, maybe we might just like expensive shoes. Whatever the reason, this is not about making judgments. It is about providing information, so here it is.

There are several positions that a former lawyer can pursue and still make six figures, and here are some of them: Director of Recruiting/Professional Development at a law firm, Director of Career Services at a law school, legal search consultant/recruiter, writer, and law school professor. These positions are within reach of many of us (unlike becoming the dean of a law school) and often seek those who have practiced law. Salary for any job, including an alternative legal job, will depend on various factors, including location. Therefore, salary will vary depending on the market in which you live. The point is that with many alternative legal careers, you will make less than you would at a large law firm but you can still make a decent living.

If the career of your choice is not available in a job working for others, consider going into business for yourself.

---

[12]WALRAA Salary Survey 2008 presented by Eva Wisnik, 4.

Consider being an entrepreneur. Being an entrepreneur is not without risks, but it is also not without rewards. Remember, you have skills—transferable skills. As an attorney, you are a writer, a speaker, and analytical, at the very least. If you are like some attorneys, you might not even want to use lawyering skills anymore and that is why you are looking for an alternative. You can learn new skills for whatever interests you.

Some of the same techniques mentioned in this chapter apply whether you are preparing for an alternative job working for someone else or an alternative business working for yourself. For example, if you want to be a career advisor working in career services in a law school, I would recommend that you get involved with things while still being an attorney that show your interest in career advising. I would suggest that you maybe get involved in firm recruiting and write articles about legal careers. If you wanted to become a career coach, working for yourself, you could also get involved in firm recruiting and write articles about legal careers. Whether you are applying for a job in career services or creating marketing materials for your new career coaching business you would still need to take what is in your resume to get an attorney job and tailor it for your new career. If you have your own business, you probably would not use a resume, but your marketing materials would probably contain some of the same information. For a book that might inspire you to be an entrepreneur, see *The Big Idea: How to Make Your Entrepreneurial Dreams Come True, From the Aha Moment to Your First Million* by Donny Deutsch and Catherine Whitney.

Remember, no matter what career you choose, there is no one path to success and obtaining the career of your dreams. Also, remember that you can change your mind and do not have to stick to one career path the entire length of your career. Do not feel that you are a failure because you have changed your mind more than once about how to use your law degree. A career is a journey—something even this Type A personality had to learn. Pursue the career that you feel will make you happy. And if it doesn't make you happy, pursue another career—in or outside of the law—while knowing that obtaining a law degree has helped to prepare you for the career of your dreams—whatever that may be.

Chapter Sixteen

What to Do if You've Been Laid Off

You get a knock on your door and your partner/mentor comes in and closes the door. "I know that you've heard that the firm hasn't done as well this quarter as it did last quarter. You know that your work is stellar, and you are a good fit for the firm, but given the downturn in the economy and the fact that you are in the mortgage-backed securities practice group, we are sorry but we are going to have to let you go." What should you do?

Start to Heal

Let me be one of the first to say, "I'm sorry." This is not easy emotionally or financially, but don't blame yourself. You might wonder why you were let go and not others. Don't dwell on this. You are having to leave your comfort zone, possibly friends, and your livelihood, and it wasn't even your own decision. It might have even occurred without warning. It's not fair, but you have options. There is hope.

Attitude is everything. You can't go into interviews with a sad and deflated attitude, and you shouldn't because you have nothing to be ashamed of. If you need help coping because it is natural to feel bad or even depressed after a layoff, get help. Talk to a counselor, or career coach, or support group, or friends, or family—whatever works for you.

A Firm Understanding

Ask your firm[13] what it is offering to you since you have been laid off. Does your firm offer severance? Will your firm provide a counselor? What will your firm say about you when called or asked why you left? Does your firm offer free outplacement services? Use them. Outplacement services can appear in many forms, but they include services such as job search assistance, resume review, interview preparation, and other related services. If your firm has not let you know about any outplacement services, ask your firm if it is willing to offer any outplacement services.

Where are the Jobs? Finding Openings

Although the economy is not in great shape, and many employers are laying off attorneys, some employers are still hiring attorneys. If you worked at one type of entity, apply for job openings at other types of entities in addition to the type of entity you just left. For example, if you worked at a firm, consider applying to government positions or positions in corporations. As stated earlier in this book, job openings may be found in various places; however, do not limit yourself to apply only to posted jobs. See the chapter in this book entitled "Where are the Jobs?: Searching for Job Openings."

---

[13] Although this chapter is primarily written as if giving advice to someone who has been laid off from a law firm, much of the advice in this chapter can be helpful to any lawyer who has been laid off whether his or her employer is a law firm, government agency, or some other type of employer.

Network

Network, network, network. Given that in an economy such as this, there are more people applying for jobs than job openings, you need every advantage you can obtain. If there are two equally impressive resumes, and one is sent to the hiring partner directly from the candidate, and the other is hand-delivered from a partner in that firm with a recommendation that "I know her and she would be an excellent addition to the firm," who do you think is more likely to get the interview?— the woman with the hand-delivered resume. Also, by networking, you will let people know that you are looking for a job, and you will be able to find out about even more job openings than you would by merely searching the Internet. Many job openings are not posted even in this Internet Age. For more about networking, see the chapter entitled "Who Do You Know?: Networking."

Your Resume

If you haven't already done so, update your resume. Make sure that your resume is as close to perfect as possible. Have someone in the career services office in your law school to review it or a friend if your law school doesn't offer this service. Competition demands an excellent resume in form and content and given the state of the economy, there are more candidates for fewer jobs—competition is great.

Tell the truth on the entire resume. Specifically, make sure that the time period of your employment is accurate. On your resume, put the month and year of your last day at the firm. Don't say that you presently work at your former firm if you have left. For example, if you started at the firm on August

1, 2004 and your last day on the job was April 15, 2008, list this job's time period as "August 2004 – April 2008." Do not list it as "August 2004 – Present." That is a lie. For more about resumes, see the chapter entitled "Who am I?: Your Resume."

The Interview

Be prepared to answer why you left the firm. Tell the truth. Explain that you were laid off for the reasons told to you (e.g., that due to the economic downturn, you were laid off). It would be good to have references that will support the reasons that you give as to why you were laid off. It would also be good to have references of people you worked with that can intelligently speak about your work, hopefully in a positive manner. Know too that you can have, and probably do have, more than one reason for applying for the job.

Ask yourself: If you had not been laid off and you were interviewing, how would you answer, "Why are you applying for this job?" Add the answer to that question to your statement about being laid off. For example, say that you are applying to be an Assistant Director of Career Services at a law school and you are asked "Why did you leave your previous job?" One possible answer: "I was one of 75 associates laid off from my law firm because business was extremely slow in my practice group after the downturn in the economy. However, I have wanted to work in a legal career services office for a while because of my interest in helping others to secure jobs in the legal field. I was on the Recruiting Committee of the law firm, often interviewed candidates for associate positions, and I often enjoyed helping other colleagues answer questions about their careers." Make sure that the reasons that you give for wanting the position are true. A dishonest answer is well, dishonest, and if your answers do not ring true, a good interviewer will be able to tell.

If telling the truth is not a compelling reason in and of itself, there is another reason to disclose that you have been laid off when asked why you left the firm. If one of your references is from your previous employer, the employer with which you are interviewing will more than likely contact your previous employer and find out that you were laid off. Even if you do not list someone from your prior firm as one of your references, your possible new employer might want to contact your old firm, and if he or she does this, again, he or she could find out that you were laid off. The fact that you did not disclose that you were laid off will become a bigger issue than your being laid off and could keep you from getting the job. Of course, there is always the risk that someone will unfairly hold the fact that you were laid off against you, but I think that anyone who does that is not professional. You were laid off because of economic reasons, not job performance. For more about interviews, see the chapter entitled "Interview."

I Haven't Found a Job Yet, Now What?

Do temporary or contract work in the interim while you continue to search for a job. You can offer your services on a contract basis either directly to an employer or indirectly by offering your services through a temporary agency. Employers might be interested in hiring you on a contract basis in this economy because it is a temporary arrangement, your rate per hour will more than likely be less than the hourly equivalent of hiring you in a salaried position, and the employer usually will not have to provide benefits to you.

If you need health insurance, the Consolidated Omnibus Budget Reconciliation Act (or COBRA) "provides certain former employees, retirees, spouses, former spouses, and dependent children the right to temporary continuation of health coverage at group rates."[14] Obtaining health insurance through COBRA can be expensive, but its cost has decreased due to the American Recovery and Reinvestment Act of 2009. Now,

> [e]ligible individuals pay only 35 percent of their COBRA premiums and the remaining 65 percent is reimbursed to the coverage provider through a tax credit. The premium reduction applies to periods of health coverage beginning on or after February 17, 2009 and lasts for up to nine months for those eligible for COBRA during the period beginning September 1, 2008 and ending December 31, 2009 due to an involuntary termination of employment that occurred during that period.[15]

If COBRA is too expensive, consider getting your own health insurance policy. See Web sites such as www.ehealthinsurance .com which lists various health insurance plans for individuals and families, allows you to compare these plans online, allows you to apply for a plan online, and has advisors that can help you over the telephone. Also check to see if you local bar offers health insurance. For example, the DC Bar offers health insurance to its members.

---

[14]"FAQs For Employees About COBRA Continuation Health Coverage," U.S. Department of Labor, http://www.dol.gov/ebsa/faqs/faq_consumer_cobra.html (accessed May 18, 2009).

[15] "COBRA Continuation Coverage Assistance Under The American Recovery And Reinvestment Act of 2009," U.S. Department of Labor, http://www.dol.gov/ebsa/COBRA.html (accessed May 18, 2009).

If you have student loans and you can't make your payments, contact the holders of your student loan to see what options you have and the consequences of those options. For example, see if you can get a forbearance on your student loan until you can find a job or start to make payments again. However, know the consequences. For example, interest will probably still accrue while the loan is in forbearance and will be added to the principal balance of your loan at the end of the forbearance period, so that when you start making payments again, your payments will be higher.

What's the Alternative—Alternative Job That Is?

Consider a job outside of law. If you were thinking of doing something different, now is the time. Consider alternative careers within law if you are not ready to abandon law altogether. For information about the alternative career job search, see the chapter entitled "What's the Alternative?: The Alternative Career Job Search."

Unemployedlawyers.com

For a Web site dedicated to unemployed lawyers and legal staff see www.site.unemployedlawyers.com/. The Web site contains links to Web sites that can be useful to lawyers such as links to recruiters, temporary and contract staffing agencies, career counselors, associations, federal courts and agencies, and law firms. The Web site also provides other helpful information such as job hunting tips, seminar opportunities, and articles.

Chapter Seventeen

Don't Give Up

Looking for a job can be heartbreaking and disappointing and make you doubt yourself as you receive rejections from potential employers, but don't give up. An employer can have a vast amount of reasons why he or she may not choose you for the position, many of which may have nothing to do with you. For example, the employer might think that you are overqualified for the position even if you are not. Whatever the reason, do not dwell on your not getting this job unless you are not receiving any offers of employment. Even then, there could be other reasons such as a soft job market. However, you must balance not obsessing over why you did not get a job with honest, self-reflection. If you are going on several interviews and not getting job offers, it could be that you are not interviewing well, for example. Consult your law school career services office or your coach, if you have one. Possibly, have a mock interview if you have not or another mock interview if you have had one.

But, don't give up. Charlotte E. Ray was born in 1850[16]—a time when African-Americans were slaves; however, Charlotte E. Ray did not give up in this era of slavery and segregation. In 1872, only a few years after the end of the Civil War, Charlotte E. Ray became the first African-American

---

[16] *Encyclopaedia Britannica Online*, s.v. "Ray, Charlotte E.," www.britannica.com/EBchecked/topic/492386/Charlotte-E-Ray (accessed May 18, 2009).

female lawyer.[17] Sandra Day O'Connor graduated from
Stanford Law School in 1952 and the only job offer she could
receive from a law firm was for a legal secretary position, but
she didn't give up—she took a position as a deputy district
attorney in San Mateo County, California and years later, she
became the first woman appointed to the United States Supreme
Court.[18]

Some of you will read this book and proclaim that I
don't know what I am talking about because only the top 10
percent of the top 10 schools get jobs; that what is in this book
is obvious; that you have been trying to get a job, have used all
or some of the techniques mentioned in this book, and still don't
have a job; that life is unfair; and the world is a mean place.
Well, even if all of this is true, you still need a job at the end of
the day, and a negative attitude will not help. If you have a
negative attitude, you will almost certainly hurt your chances of
getting a job. A negative attitude comes through in your
interview. See "Attitude is Everything" in the chapter of this
book entitled "Interview."

I know it's hard when you want something or need
something and can't get it—I've been there. I can't even
imagine how tough it must be to need a job when your family
depends on you. The stress and pressure of that must be
enormous. But, try not to let the job search process get you
down. Don't remain isolated. Talk to others searching for a job

[17]J. Clay Smith Jr., ed., *Rebels in Law: Voices in History of Black Women
Lawyers* (Ann Arbor: The University of Michigan Press, 2000), 277.
[18]*Encyclopaedia Britannica Online, Encyclopaedia Britannica Profiles –
300 WOMEN WHO CHANGED THE WORLD*, s.v. "O'Connor, Sandra
Day" (by Brian P. Smentkowski), www.britannica.com/women/article-
9056723 (accessed May 19, 2009).

just like you are, or talk to a coach, career counselor, or career services personnel. Talk with your support system (e.g., friends and family). Write in a journal or write on a blog. Join a support group. However, when discussing your job search in any of these methods, make sure that the individuals can be discreet if your search is not a public search. Or, if writing on a blog for example, don't use any identifying information such as your real name. All of these or none of these might work for you—do what works for you and whatever helps you feel hopeful and positive. Don't give up.

Remember, you made it through 3 years of law school. You can secure a job that you want. I can't say it enough—don't give up.

CONGRATULATIONS!!
Now the Real Work Begins

Now that you have done everything right (i.e., followed the advice in this book to the letter (smile)), you have received a job offer at a salary and benefits that you want and with all other parameters as you want them. You have accepted the job—and—now the real work begins—the actual job. This might be the job that you always wanted—your "dream job"—or a stop on the way to your "dream job." Don't lose heart if after working at this new job you are searching the trunk of your car for this book to read again and start another job search. You should continue to search, not just for a job, but for your passion—something that you would do for free if only your landlord and the rest of the world didn't require money. I used to feel somewhat like a loser for having had different jobs until a wise person pointed out to me that a career is a journey, with twists and turns that ultimately lead you to what you are really supposed to do, whatever that may be.

My winding path led me to writing and I couldn't be happier. I hope that this book helps to make your job search a little easier, getting you closer to the job you want and ultimately, closer to your true calling. I know, it's just a job search guide, but a girl can hope. Happy Job Hunting!

Appendix A
Internet Web Sites

The following is a list of Internet Web sites where you can find job openings in the legal industry:

- LawJobs.com (www.lawjobs.com)(various legal jobs in all of the states in the United States of America)

- Law Firm Web sites (e.g., www.arnoldporter.com)(Choose "CAREERS.")(attorney and administrative positions such as professional development manager)

- USAJOBS (www.usajobs.opm.gov)(jobs with the federal government of the United States of America)

- Federal Government Agency Web sites (e.g., www.usdoj.gov)(Choose "JOBS.")

- State Web sites (e.g., www.virginia.gov)(Choose "Employment.")

- Federal Court Web sites (e.g., United States Court of Appeals, Eleventh Circuit, www.ca11.uscourts.gov/hr/index.php)

- State Court Web sites (e.g., New Jersey, www.judiciary.state.nj.us/jobs/index.htm)

- NALP (www.nalp.org)(Choose "Jobs.")(legal career positions such as in recruiting or professional development in a law firm or career services at a law school)

- Law School/College/University Web sites (e.g., www.vanderbilt.edu)(Choose "Jobs.")(Job openings at a law school can appear on a college, university, or law school Web site.)

- Law School Job Databases (usually open to students and alumni only)

- PSLawNet (www.pslawnet.org)(See the "JOB SEEKER" section on the PSLawNet home page.)(a public service law network; has an online database that provides information on public interest organizations and public interest job opportunities for lawyers and law students; contact your law school career services office for access)

- Monster.com (www.monster.com)(various jobs in the United States of America and countries around the world)

- careerbuilder.com (www.careerbuilder.com)(various jobs in the United States of America and countries around the world)

- Indeed (www.indeed.com)(various jobs in the United States of America and countries around the world)

- Simply Hired (www.simplyhired.com)(various jobs in the United States of America and countries around the world)

- American Bar Association (www.abanet.org)(Choose "Member Resources." Next, choose "Jobs for Lawyers" or "Jobs at the ABA" listed under "Career Resources," which is listed under "Professional Development." There are several links to job search databases including the ABA-CLE Career Counsel Jobs Page (www.abanet.org/careercounsel/jobs.html).)

- ACC (Association of Corporate Counsel)(www.acc.com) (Choose "Careers.")(provides job openings for attorney positions, including in-house positions at corporations in the United States of America and countries around the world)

- MCCA (Minority Corporate Counsel Association) (www.mcca.com)(Choose "Career Center.")(provides job openings for attorney positions, including in-house positions at corporations in the United States of America and countries around the world)

- Corporations' Web sites (e.g., www.microsoft.com/careers/)

- District Attorney and Public Defender Web Sites (e.g., www.manhattanda.org/careers/ (New York County District Attorney's Office))(provides information about career opportunities with this office)

- Wisnik Career Enterprises, Inc. (www.wisnik.com)(Choose "Jobs For Recruiters," or "Jobs for Marketing Professionals," or "Jobs for Practice Managers" depending on your interest.)(training and placement firm that places individuals in legal recruitment, marketing, and law practice manager positions)

- craigslist (e.g., chicago.craigslist.org (craigslist listings for Chicago))(various jobs in the United States of America and countries around the world)

- HG.org (http://www.hg.org/law-jobs.asp)(various legal jobs in the United States of America and countries around the world)

- Darling Hill (www.darlinghill.com/category/jobs)(posts what the Web site considers to be "flexible lawyer jobs")

This is just a small sampling of the Web sites that contain job openings in the legal industry. Not every place that you want to work will have a Web site with job postings; however, many will. In addition to searching Web sites dedicated to providing job postings, if you know of places where you want to work, look at their Web sites for open positions. Do not rely on Web sites alone—many jobs are never posted. It will take a combination of job postings, networking, and other methods to find out about job openings.

There are some Web sites where you have to pay a fee to access the jobs database (e.g., www.lawcrossing.com). I have not used these services for my own job searches. Try the free services and Web sites first. If you do decide to use one of these fee-based services, try to get a free trial period to see if it is for you. If you can't get a free trial period yourself, see if you can get a free trial period through your law school.

Appendix B
Newspapers

The following is a list of newspapers and other publications where you can find job openings in the legal industry. Note that some of these newspapers come in paper form as well as have a Web site. The paper format of the newspaper may contain job advertisements different from what may be found online. If you have access to the paper format, check it in addition to the Web site just in case each contains different job opportunities. Also note that although many of these newspapers are specific to a certain location, or published in a certain city (listed below in parenthesis next to the names of the newspapers), some of these newspapers will list job openings for other locations in addition to the location for that newspaper. For example, the *Virginia Lawyers Weekly* lists job openings in Virginia but also contains job postings from other states such as Massachusetts and North Carolina.

- *Legal Times* (Washington, DC)(www.law.com/jsp/dc/ index.jsp)(Choose "Classifieds" to be linked to the Law.com LawJobs Web site.)

- *Daily Report* (often referred to as the *Fulton County Daily Report*)(Atlanta, Georgia)(www.dailyreportonline.com) (Click on "Search Jobs" to be linked to the Law.com LawJobs Web site.)

- *The Daily Record* (Maryland)(www.mddailyrecord.com) (Choose "Classified," "Employment," and then select "Attorney" or "Legal." Note that you can choose "Refine Search" to choose other parameters such as looking for job ads in issues of the paper from other dates.)

- *Virginia Lawyers Weekly* (Virginia)(Virginia, but also job postings from other states such as Massachusetts and North Carolina)(www.valawyersweekly.com)(Choose "CLASSIFIEDS" – "Find a Job." Once you have done this, to search the databases, choose "Legal Classifieds" – "Jobs.")

- *New York Law Journal* (New York)(www.law.com/jsp/nylj/index.jsp)(Choose "Jobs" listed under "LAW.COM NETWORK – SITES" to be linked to the Law.com LawJobs Web site. You can also choose "MORE JOBS," listed under "lawjobs.com" on the *New York Law Journal* Home page, to obtain a list of openings in the state of New York.)

- *The Chronicle of Higher Education* (United States of America and countries around the world)(chronicle.com) (Choose "Careers.")(law school professor and law school administration positions as well as positions at colleges and universities)

- *The Washington Post* (Washington, DC) (www.washingtonpost.com/)(Choose "JOBS.")

- *The New York Times* (New York, New York) (www.nytimes.com/)(Choose "JOBS.")

- *The Atlanta Journal-Constitution* (Atlanta, Georgia) (www.ajc.com/?cxntlid=nav_hme)(Choose "Jobs.")

- *The Legal Intelligencer* (Pennsylvania) (www.law.com/jsp/pa/index.jsp)(Choose "Jobs" listed under "Classifieds" to be linked to the Law.com LawJobs Web site.)

- *Pennsylvania Law Weekly* (Pennsylvania) (www.palawweekly.com/plw/default.aspx)(Choose

"Classifieds" to be linked to the Law.com LawJobs Web site.)

- *The Philadelphia Inquirer* (Philadelphia, Pennsylvania) (www.philly.com/inquirer/)(Choose "Jobs.")

- *San Francisco Chronicle* (San Francisco, California)(www.sfgate.com/chronicle/)(Choose "Jobs" listed under "CHRONICLE CLASSIFIEDS.")

- *The Recorder* (California)(A Web site produced by the same team behind this daily legal newspaper is "Cal Law" – www.law.com/jsp/ca/index.jsp.)(Choose "find a job" to be linked to the LawJobs Web site on Law.com.)

- *Los Angeles Times* (Los Angeles, California) (www.latimes.com/)(Choose "Jobs.")

- *Chicago Daily Law Bulletin* (Chicago, Illinois) (www.chicagolawbulletin.com/browser_pass.cfm)(Choose "Jobs.")

- *Chicago Tribune* (Chicago, Illinois) (www.chicagotribune.com/)(Choose "Jobs.")

- *Chicago Sun-Times* (Chicago, Illinois) (www.suntimes.com/index.html)(Choose "Classifieds," then choose "Careers.")

- *The Boston Globe* (Boston, Massachusetts) (www.boston.com/bostonglobe)(Choose "JOBS.")

- *The Denver Post* (Denver, Colorado) (www.denverpost.com/)(Choose "JOBS.")

- *The Seattle Times* (Seattle, Washington) (http://seattletimes.nwsource.com/html/home/index.html) (Choose "Jobs.")

- *The Miami Herald* (Miami, Florida) (www.miamiherald.com/)(Choose "JOBS.")

- *Daily Business Review* (South Florida – Miami–Dade, Broward, and Palm Beach counties) (www.dailybusinessreview.com)(Choose "Employment" to be linked to the Law.com LawJobs.com Web site.)

- *The News & Observer* (regional newspaper in North Carolina with the main office located in Raleigh, North Carolina)(www.newsobserver.com/)(Choose "Jobs.")

- *Connecticut Law Tribune* (Connecticut) (www.ctlawtribune.com/)(Choose "FIND A JOB" to be linked to the Law.com LawJobs Web site.)

- *Delaware Law Weekly* (Delaware) (www.delawarelawweekly.com/)(refers you to LawJobs.com)

- *New Jersey Law Journal* (New Jersey) (www.law.com/jsp/nj/index.jsp)(Choose "FIND A JOB" to be linked to the Law.com LawJobs Web site.)

- *Texas Lawyer* (Texas)(www.texaslawyer.com or www.law.com/jsp/tx/index.jsp)(Choose "Jobs" located under "LAW.COM NETWORK – SITES" to be linked to the Law.com LawJobs Web site.)

- *Minnesota Lawyer* (Minneapolis, Minnesota) (www.minnlawyer.com/index.cfm)(Choose "Classifieds" and then choose "Employment.")

- AALS *Placement Bulletin* (United States of America and countries around the world)(The AALS is the Association of American Law Schools. It publishes the *Placement Bulletin* that lists available law school faculty and administrative positions and job openings related to legal education in schools other than law schools.)

This is just a small sampling of the newspapers and publications that contain job openings in the legal industry. Look for local newspapers and local legal industry newspapers. Since local newspapers and local legal industry newspapers often contain open positions within the legal profession, more than likely, your local newspapers will contain positions for your geographic area. Additionally, these newspapers might contain open positions that would not otherwise be found in the national newspapers.

Note that some of these newspapers online are links to national job search boards such as careerbuilder.com, or Yahoo!, or LawJobs.com. However, even when linking to the national job search boards, by going through some of the specific newspapers, the job search is automatically narrowed for you. For example, by searching using *The Denver Post*, the Web site takes you to Yahoo!'s job search page, but Denver, Colorado is already in the "Location" search box and "Include Surrounding Cities" is selected.

Appendix C
Associations, Groups in the Legal Industry

The following is a list of associations and groups in the legal industry:

- American Bar Association (ABA)
- State Bar Association (e.g., Tennessee Bar Association)
- Local Bar Association (e.g., Chicago Bar Association)
- National Bar Association (NBA)
- Hispanic National Bar Association (HNBA)
- National Asian Pacific American Bar Association (NAPABA)
- National Native American Bar Association (NNABA)
- Federal Bar Association (FBA)
- NALP (Association for Legal Career Professionals)
- Washington Area Legal Recruitment Administrators Association (WALRAA)
- Association of Corporate Counsel (ACC)
- Minority Corporate Counsel Association (MCCA)
- Association of American Law Schools (AALS)
- National District Attorneys Association (NDAA)
- Public Law Section of the State Bar of California
- The Florida Bar, Government Lawyer Section
- American Bar Association – Government and Public Sector Lawyers Division

- American Health Lawyers Association (AHLA)
- American Immigration Lawyers Association (AILA)

For a list of other legal associations, and links to the Web sites of those associations, see www.findlaw.com/06associations/index.html. For information about state and local bar associations, see www.abanet.org/barserv/stlobar.html.

Appendix D
Legal Recruiters

Legal Recruiters/Legal Search Consultants

- For a list of legal recruiters or legal search consultants, see the NALSC's (National Association of Legal Search Consultants) Web site which contains a membership directory: www.nalsc.org/membership/directory.cfm.

- When I used legal search consultants, I had good experiences working with Major, Lindsey & Africa and hughes CONSULTANTS LLC.

- BCG Attorney Search is another legal recruiting firm. According to its Web site, it is "dedicated exclusively to placing top associates and partners in premier law firms."[19]

- For a placement firm that places individuals in legal recruitment, marketing, and law practice manager positions, check out Wisnik Career Enterprises, Inc.

Articles About Selecting and Working with Legal Recruiters

- "FAQ about Legal Recruiting," by Stephen E. Seckler on BCG Attorney Search Web site (www.bcgsearch.com/article/60401/609/FAQ-about-Legal-Recruiting)

- "How do I go about finding a good recruiter to work with?," by Ann Israel, *New York Law Journal*, August 23, 2006, Advice for the Lawlorn on Law.com (www.law.com/jsp/law/careercenter/lawArticleCareerCente

---

[19] "ABOUT US," BCG Attorney Search, www.bcgsearch.com/aboutus.php (accessed May 19, 2009).

r.jsp?id=900005550789&How_do_I_go_about_finding_a_g
ood_recruiter_to_work_with)

- "I didn't hear from a firm when I used a headhunter. Now that I await an offer from it, the headhunter claims a fee.," by Ann Israel, *New York Law Journal*, April 5, 2006, Advice for the Lawlorn on Law.com (http://www.law.com/jsp/law/careercenter/lawArticleCareer Center.jsp?id=900005548520&I_didnt_hear_from_a_firm_ when_I_used_a_headhunter_Now_that_I_await_an_offer_fr om_it_the_headhunter_claims_a_fee)

- "Can I hire a headhunter to find a job for me? The legal recruiters I have encountered work only for the employers.," by Ann Israel, *New York Law Journal*, March 22, 2006, Advice for the Lawlorn on Law.com (www.law.com/jsp/law/careercenter/lawArticleCareerCente r.jsp?id=900005548270&Can_I_hire_a_headhunter_to_find _a_job_for_me_The_legal_recruiters_I_have_encountered_ work_only_for_the_employers).

- For more articles concerning legal recruiters, see LawJobs.com (www.law.com/jsp/law/careercenter/advice .jsp) and the BCG Attorney Search Web site (www.bcgsearch.com/ - Choose "RECENT ARTICLES" after determining which of the "RESOURCES" would be most helpful to you (e.g., "ASSOCIATE RESOURCES" or "PARTNER RESOURCES").).

Appendix E
Possible Informational Interview Questions

For the following questions, assume that the informational interviewer wants to be a district attorney. These questions can be adapted to the position you are seeking.

1. How did you become a district attorney?

2. What steps would you suggest that I take given my interest in becoming a district attorney?

3. What do you like about being a district attorney?

4. What do you dislike about being a district attorney?

5. If you are still in law school, you could ask: a. What classes do you suggest that I take in law school? b. What internships or summer jobs should I pursue?

6. What is a typical day for you, if such a day exists?

7. What skills would a district attorney need to do her job well?

8. What are good resources for looking for a job as a district attorney?

9. What groups or associations would you recommend joining?

10. Why did you become a district attorney?

11. What would you emphasize on your resume when applying for a district attorney position?

12. If the person with whom you are speaking works in an office where you cannot obtain job application information (e.g., the information is not on the office's Web site or you

can't get the information from your law school career services office), ask: What is the best procedure for applying for a position? Even if you have this information, you can still ask what is the best way to apply for the job. If you have the information, you might want to indicate that fact so that it doesn't seem like you haven't done your homework. For example: "I saw that your organization's Web site provides that I should e-mail my resume and cover letter to the Director of Legal Hiring. Is that the best way to apply for a position?" (*Questions 11 and 12 might provide an opening for the informational interviewee to ask to see your resume or even pass it along for job openings. This might also lead the informational interviewee to discuss how his office hires—again, another possible opening for asking for your resume to help you apply at his office.*)

13. How did you obtain your current position?

14. What was your interview for your current position like? Is this a typical interview for a district attorney position?

15. Ask any question for which you want an answer and cannot readily discover yourself.

Appendix F
Job Search Chart

Name of Entity	Date Resume/Application Sent	Position Sought	Status	Comments
ABC Law Firm	February 2, 2009	Associate	Resume Received	Sent resume and transcript to Walter Coleman
DEF, Inc.	February 9, 2009	Staff Attorney		Sent resume to Jo Beth Collins

Appendix G
Possible Interview Questions

Questions You May Be Asked

1. Why are you applying for this job?
2. Why are you interested in working for this organization?
3. What is your greatest strength?
4. What is your greatest weakness?
5. Where do you see yourself in 5 years? Where do you see yourself in 10 years?
6. If you couldn't practice law, what else would you do?
7. Why are you interviewing with our particular [agency, firm, corporation, organization, office]?
8. How will your current position prepare you for this position?
9. Tell me about yourself.
10. What is your salary requirement?
11. If hired, when could you start work?
12. If you do not get this job, would you be interested in other positions here?
13. Why are you leaving your current position?
14. Tell me more about [any item on your resume] on your resume.
15. Why should I hire you?
16. What are you looking for in a work place?

17. Explain a time when you were faced with a problem and how you solved the problem.

18. Why did you go to law school?

19. If you have gaps in time in your resume: What did you do during [gap in time in employment]?

20. If you are searching for a job outside of your current city of residence: Why are you moving to [insert city]?

Questions You Could Ask

I think that you should ask questions that are important to you and for which you need answers as long as you could not find out that information from another source such as the employer's Web site. Asking questions can demonstrate your knowledge about the employer and the job for which you are applying. However, only ask questions for which you are comfortable asking and for which you are prepared to discuss the topic you have brought up by asking the question. For example, you might feel that it will make you seem intelligent if while interviewing at the Public Defender's Office, you mention a recent high profile case that the Public Defender's Office won because you saw the headline in the newspaper on your commute to the interview. I hope you read the article, because, if you cannot intelligently discuss the case, you should not bring the case up. Even if you read the newspaper article, if you are not well-versed in criminal law, you might alert the interviewer to that fact which will not help your cause of securing a job offer.

Do research about the employer so that your questions can be based on real facts about the employer. This will make your questions more substantive. This will help you get answers that could affect your decision. This will also demonstrate that you have done your research. Research the people with whom you will interview, if possible. For some employers, you will be able to get biographies on the individuals on the employer's Web site, or try to see if they are in Martindale-Hubbell on martindale.com. Or, search for information on the individuals on Google. Remember that you are interviewing the employer as well, so use this opportunity to ask questions that can help you to determine if you want to have these individuals as colleagues.

Here are some of the questions you could ask in an interview:

1. What skills would a lawyer need to be successful at your firm [government agency, corporation, etcetera][20]? This question, once answered can give you the opportunity to mention your strengths. For example, if the interviewer says that to be successful at the firm, you must be a team player given the deadlines one faces, you could give an example of your pitching in to help the team: "I understand what you mean. In my last position, we had to file a motion seeking emergency relief and even though it was not my case, I was happy to help by researching the requirements for filing such a motion in the Fifth Circuit Court of Appeals. We met the deadline and won the motion. It was a great feeling to help the team, and I learned a new skill in the process."

---

[20] I will use the terms "firm" and "associate" for the rest of the questions you can ask, but you can change those terms to fit wherever you are interviewing, and most of the questions will remain relevant. For example, you can change "firm" to "government agency" and "associate" to "staff attorney."

2. Where do you see the firm being strategically in five years?

3. I read about your pro bono program where you allow associates to work on pro bono matters. Would that include work on the state's Innocence Project?

4. Does an associate work on matters across practice groups or once in a practice group, does the associate work only in that group?

5. What type of matters could an associate expect to work on in the Corporate [Litigation, Intellectual Property, Environmental, Real Estate, *etcetera*] group?

6. How do employees obtain work assignments? Is there a formal process or an informal process?

7. I understand that the firm offers training and professional development. Could you tell me more about those opportunities?

8. Ask questions particular to the interviewer: I understand that you practice [Corporate, for example] law. Could you tell me more about your practice? Why did you go to law school?

9. What expectations would you have of me if hired?

10. What is the next step in the interviewing process? Try to get a firm date that you will be contacted in the next step in the process. For more details on this subject, see the chapter in this book entitled "Follow-up."

See also *What Color is Your Parachute?2006: A Practical Manual for Job-Hunters and Career-Changers* by Richard Nelson Bolles at pages 288-289 for answers you should seek in your interview[21] and *Career Coaching: An Insider's Guide* by Marcia Bench at page 263 for questions you can ask in an interview.[22]

Questions for Which You Want the Answer But Might Not Want to Ask in the Interview

There are some questions for which you want an answer, but you might not want to ask in an interview. I would avoid asking these questions in an interview in most cases, but, as I keep saying, if you want to ask these questions, please do so. You can still get the answers to these questions without bringing them up in an interview. Ask your law school career services office, former employees of the place where you are interviewing (as long as the employees can be discreet), or current employees of the place where you are interviewing (as long as the employees can be discreet). You might also look for information on the Internet. Remember, with all of these sources, the information is only as good as the source. These questions are not bad questions, they might just be questions you would not want to ask in an interview for different reasons. For example, you might not ask a question in an interview because you might get more information in a non-interview setting (e.g., "Are employees happy here?"). Or, maybe you don't ask a question because to do so might make you and the interviewer uncomfortable and might not place you in the best

---

[21] This book is revised each year and there is a 2009 edition.
[22] A second edition of *Career Coaching: An Insider's Guide* has been written—*Career Coaching: An Insider's Guide-Second Edition* by Marcia A. Bench.

light (e.g., "Is this a sweat shop?"). Or, maybe there is a strategic reason not to ask a question (e.g., asking about salary might lead to the interviewer asking you about your salary requirements and you might price yourself out of the job).

Here are some of the questions:

1. What is the turnover rate at this place of employment?
2. How are [women, men, African-Americans, Asian-Americans, [other groups]] treated at this employer? Are there opportunities for success for these groups?
3. What is the salary for this position? This is something that you will know eventually but might not want to discuss in the first interview. To get this information earlier rather than later, it is a question you could ask in the interview or investigate through other sources. See the chapter in this book entitled "Salary."
4. Is this a sweatshop?
5. Are employees happy here?
6. Why have people left this employer? Why have people left the position or the type of position for which I am interviewing?
7. Is this a family-friendly employer?
8. Is there work-life balance at this employer?
9. Is the employer stable? For example, is the corporation on the verge of bankruptcy?
10. What are the people with whom I will work really like?
11. Is my potential supervisor easy or difficult to work with?
12. Will I learn anything while working for this employer?

In the end, if you want to ask a question, ask. If you don't want to ask a question, use other resources to find answers to your questions. Even if you ask these questions in your interview, for some of these questions, you might also want to ask others as well. This does not mean that you will not get an honest answer from your interviewer or interviewers, but asking this of more than one person might prove helpful because by asking several different people, in a non-interview setting, you might get a more realistic picture.

Appendix H
Other Career Books

I have not read all of these books, and this is not an endorsement for the books. This is just a list of books that discuss the job search.

- *What Can You Do With a Law Degree?: A Lawyer's Guide to Career Alternatives Inside, Outside & Around the Law, 5th Edition* by Deborah Arron

- *What Color is Your Parachute? 2009: A Practical Manual for Job-Hunters and Career-Changers* by Richard Nelson Bolles

- *Career Coaching: An Insider's Guide* by Marcia Bench (Although this is a book about career coaching, it discusses job search strategies.)[23]

- *Guerilla Tactics for Getting the Legal Job of Your Dreams, 2nd Edition* by Kimm Alayne Walton

- *The Right Moves: Job Search and Career Development Strategies for Lawyers* by Valerie A. Fontaine

- *Changing Jobs: A Handbook for Lawyers in the New Millennium, Third Edition* edited by Heidi McNeil Staudenmaier

- *Escape from Corporate America: A Practical Guide to Creating the Career of Your Dreams* by Pamela Skillings

---

[23] A second edition of *Career Coaching: An Insider's Guide* has been written—*Career Coaching: An Insider's Guide-Second Edition* by Marcia A. Bench.

Appendix I
Resources—Academic Job Search

- *The Chronicle of Higher Education* – This may be found in print or online (chronicle.com). While you must subscribe to view portions of the online version, many of the portions of the online version are for the public (i.e., those that have not subscribed to the publication). For example, you can see job postings for current job openings. The Web site contains helpful articles on topics such as academic culture, adjunct professors, conducting an academic job search, teaching, publishing, and work and family.

- Association of American Law Schools (AALS) – *Placement Bulletin* – This is a "publication that lists available faculty and administrative positions, as well as positions related to legal education outside law schools. It comes out four times each academic year."[24] To see an example of a *Placement Bulletin*, see www.aals.org/documents/pbsample.pdf.

- AALS Faculty Recruitment Conference – This is an annual event held in Washington, DC, usually in the fall, where people interested in interviewing for faculty positions primarily at law schools, if chosen to interview, may interview. The interviewing schedule can be hectic if you have several interviews. For more information about this conference, see www.aals.org/services_recruitment.php.

- Contact your law school career services office for help with your academic job search.

---

[24] "AALS Publications," AALS, www.aals.org/services_publications.php (accessed May 19, 2009).

- Speak with law professors or others with positions that you seek. Conduct informational interviews.

- HigherEdJobs.com (www.higheredjobs.com/) – lists job openings in academia. You can search by category (e.g., Faculty), type (e.g., Part-time/Adjunct), or location (e.g., State/Province). You can search by "Law and Legal Studies" after selecting "Faculty."

- "Uncloaking Law School Hiring: A Recruit's Guide to the AALS Faculty Recruitment Conference" (www.aals.org/frs/jle.php)(originally published in the *Journal of Legal Education* in 1988 but according to the AALS Web site "much of the advice is still pertinent"[25])

- *Breaking Into The Academy: The 2002-2004 Michigan Journal of Race & Law Guide for Aspiring Law Professors* edited by Gabriel J. Chin and Denise C. Morgan

- Newspapers and Web sites – Sometimes the newspapers and Web sites already mentioned in this book will list positions in academia. *See Appendix A and Appendix B for a list of Web sites and a list of newspapers.*

- Check the Web site for the school or schools in which you are interested in working. School Web sites will list open positions. The positions might not be in obvious places so check the index, and look for job openings under headings such as "Employment" or "Human Resources."

- Washington Area Legal Recruitment Administrators Association (WALRAA)(www.walraa.org)(posts openings for law school career services positions in addition to other positions)

---

[25] "FAR Advice," AALS, www.aals.org/frs/jle.php (accessed May 19, 2009).

- NALP (www.nalp.org)(posts openings for career services positions at law schools in addition to other positions)
- Careers in Law Teaching Web Page by Eric Goldman (www.ericgoldman.org/Resources/becomingalawprofessor.htm)
- *From Lawyer to Administrator* (NALP, 2006) (www.nalp.org/assets/222_fromlawyertoadministrator.pdf)
- Legal Writing Institute (www.lwionline.org/)(Choose "EMPLOYMENT LISTINGS.")(has listings for job openings for positions associated with legal writing and research programs in law schools such as legal writing instructors, professors, and directors of legal writing programs)

Appendix J
Alternative Careers for Lawyers

The following is a list of some of the alternative careers that a person with a law degree can pursue. The Web sites in parenthesis near the job titles are Web sites that you could look at to search for job openings for these types of jobs and also are places where you can often find descriptions of these types of jobs.

- Professional Development Manager (www.nalp.org/jobs)
- Professional Development Coordinator (www.nalp.org/jobs)
- Recruiting Manager (www.nalp.org/jobs)
- Recruiting Coordinator (www.nalp.org/jobs)
- Director of Career Services at a Law School (www.nalp.org/jobs)
- Assistant Director of Career Services at a Law School (www.nalp.org/jobs)
- Legal Recruiter/Search Consultant (Major, Lindsey & Africa - www.mlaglobal.com/pages/JobSearch.aspx); (BCG Attorney Search - www.bcgsearch.com/joblistings.php)
- Law Professor (chronicle.com; law school/college/ university Web sites; www.higheredjobs.com)
- Professor/Instructor of Legal Related Subjects at a College/University (chronicle.com; college/university Web sites; www.higheredjobs.com)
- Law Librarian (American Association of Law Libraries - www.aallnet.org/hotline/hotline.asp)(Note, you will probably be required in many of these positions to have a

graduate degree in library science in addition to a JD; however, there might be exceptions.)

- Knowledge Manager at a law firm (www.infocurrent.com/candidate/searchlines_jobsearch.asp)
- Knowledge Management Support Attorney (www.monster.com)
- Career Coach for Lawyers (www.nalp.org/jobs)
- Freelance Writer (www.freelancewriting.com)

Appendix K
Agencies That Provide Legal Contract Work

The following is a list of some of the agencies that provide legal temporary and contract work. Some agencies have opportunities in many locations throughout the United States (e.g., HIRECounsel and Kelly Law Registry), or the United States and other countries such as Canada (e.g., Robert Half Legal), while others focus on providing opportunities to a smaller geographic area (e.g., Palmer Legal Staffing provides opportunities in the Washington, DC metropolitan area).

- HIRECounsel (www.hirecounsel.com)
- Counsel on Call (www.counseloncall.com)
- Ajilon Legal (www.ajilonlegal.com)
- Kelly Law Registry (www.kellylawregistry.com)
- Assigned Counsel (www.assignedcounsel.com)
- JuriStaff Legal Staffing (www.juristaff.com/temporary)
- Robert Half Legal (www.roberthalflegal.com)
- Special Counsel (www.specialcounsel.com)
- Palmer Legal Staffing (www.palmerlegalstaffing.com)
- InfoCurrent (www.infocurrent.com)(provides temporary and contract opportunities in the legal library and research field)

About the Author

Erin C. Coleman is a writer who, after being in the legal field for twelve years, recently took the plunge, quitting the practice of law, to write full time. Erin's legal experience, as well as her experience as an Assistant Director of Legal Career Services, allow her to provide legal career advice based not only on research and past experience as a career advisor but also based on her personal experiences in the legal field over the past twelve years. In addition to being an Assistant Director of Legal Career Services, Erin practiced law in Tennessee as an associate at a law firm and in Georgia as an associate at a law firm. When she decided that she no longer wanted to be on the partnership track at a law firm, Erin looked for alternative ways to practice law or use her law degree. Erin was a Staff Attorney at a law firm, a Senior Assistant City Attorney for city government, a knowledge management administrator in a law firm, a contract attorney, and a Staff Lawyer at a law firm in Washington, DC.

Erin received her Bachelor of Arts, cum laude, in Business Administration from Rhodes College where she was elected to Phi Beta Kappa. Erin received her Juris Doctor from Vanderbilt University School of Law where she was a Student Writing Editor of the *Vanderbilt Journal of Transnational Law* and a member of the Vanderbilt Jessup International Moot Court Competition Team. Erin lives in the Washington, DC area.

Table of Content

Introduction to Gestational Diabetes

Mrs. Stacy was 26 weeks pregnant when she went to the doctor for her regular prenatal checkup. During the checkup, the doctor did a glucose challenge test, which is a blood test that is used to screen for gestational diabetes. Mrs. Stacy's glucose levels were high, which meant that she had gestational diabetes.

Gestational diabetes is a type of diabetes that develops during pregnancy. It is caused by a combination of hormones produced by the placenta and changes in the mother's body that make it harder for her to use insulin. Insulin is a hormone that helps the body use glucose (sugar) for energy.

Gestational diabetes can increase the risk of health problems for both the mother and the baby. For the mother, gestational diabetes can increase the risk of preeclampsia, birth defects, and cesarean section. For the baby, gestational diabetes can increase the risk of macrosomia (a baby that is too large for gestational age), hypoglycemia (low blood sugar), and respiratory problems.

The doctor told Mrs. Stacy that she could manage her gestational diabetes with a healthy diet, exercise, and sometimes insulin. Mrs. Stacy was determined to do everything she could to keep her blood sugar levels in a healthy range so that she could have a healthy pregnancy and a healthy baby.

Mrs. Stacy started by reading about gestational diabetes and healthy eating for pregnant women. She also started exercising regularly. She found that walking was a great way to get exercise and it also helped to keep her blood sugar levels in check.

Mrs. Stacy also found this unpublished cookbook from a friend that was specifically designed for women with gestational diabetes. The cookbook was full of delicious and healthy recipes that were perfect for pregnant women. Mrs. Stacy started cooking from the cookbook and she was amazed at how good the food tasted.

After a few weeks of following the cookbook's recipes, Mrs. Stacy went back to the doctor for a follow-up appointment. The doctor was pleased to see that Mrs. Stacy's blood sugar levels were in a healthy range. The doctor told Mrs. Stacy that she had done a great job of managing her gestational diabetes and that she was on track to have a healthy pregnancy and a healthy baby.

Mrs. Stacy was so happy that she had been able to reverse her gestational diabetes using a cookbook. She reached out to the writer of the cookbook and told the writer about her experience with gestational diabetes and how the cookbook had helped her manage her condition.

The writer was impressed by Stacy's story, and he agreed to publish the cookbook. The cookbook was a success, and it helped many women with gestational diabetes manage their condition and have healthy pregnancies and babies.

She was grateful for the cookbook and for the doctor's support. She knew that she would continue to follow the cookbook's recipes after her baby was born so that she could stay healthy for herself and for her family.

What is in that cookbook?

Dive in to find out...

What is Gestational Diabetes?

Gestational diabetes is a type of diabetes that develops during pregnancy. It is caused by a combination of hormones produced by the placenta and changes in the mother's body that make it harder for her to use insulin. Insulin is a hormone that helps the body use glucose (sugar) for energy.

Who is at Risk for Gestational Diabetes?

Women who are at increased risk for gestational diabetes include:

- Women who are overweight or obese
- Women who have a family history of diabetes
- Women who have had gestational diabetes in a previous pregnancy
- Women who have had a baby that was large for gestational age
- Women who have had a miscarriage or stillbirth
- Women who have high blood pressure or preeclampsia
- Women who have polycystic ovary syndrome (PCOS)